Gift of God

A 90-Day Devotional

Gift of God

Daily Words of Encouragement and Hope

Joanie Shawhan

Gift of God

www.joanieshawhan.com
Published by Graceleaf Publishing
ISBN: 979-8-9997127-1-4

"Anna Joy" is a pseudonym to protect the privacy of those integral to her story, which is told in *Song of Joy: A Little Girl in the Hands of a Big God*, Graceleaf Publishing, 2025.

This devotional is dedicated to our
spiritual mothers and fathers.
Thank you for your encouragement,
prayers, teaching us the Scriptures,
and showing us how to pray.

Contents

Day 29 Joshua 1:9

Day 30 Isaiah 28:16

Day 31 John 17:23

Day 32 1 John 1:7

Day 33 Psalm 21:6

Day 34 James 1:2–4

Day 35 Exodus 8:23

Day 36 John 7:38

Day 37 Romans 8:37

Day 38 Hebrews 3:4

Day 39 1 Thessalonians 3:13

Day 40 John 16:33

Day 41 Romans 12:21

Day 42 Ephesians 1:11

Day 43 Matthew 26:41

Day 44 John 17:16

Day 45 1 Corinthians 13:4–5

Day 46 Proverbs 3:5–6

Day 47 John 17:13

Day 48 Psalm 61:2

Day 49 1 Corinthians 2:9

Day 50 Luke 12:11–12

Day 51 Philippians 4:13

Day 52 Hebrews 12:1–2

Day 53 2 Corinthians 12:9

Day 54 John 3:14–15

Day 55 Acts 17:26–28

Day 56 Job 16:19–21

Day 57 Isaiah 41:10

Day 58 Hebrews 13:5

Day 59 Psalm 27:1

Day 60 Psalm 32:7

Day 61 Song of Songs 4:7

Day 62 Proverbs 8:34–35

Day 63 Ephesians 6:12

Day 64 Psalm 2:4

Day 65 John 10:27–28

Day 66 Ephesians 3:10

Day 67 Luke 18:1

Day 68 Luke 15:10

Day 69 Philippians 4:19

Day 70 1 John 3:7

Day 71 John 12:32

Day 72 Psalm 82:4

Day 73 Acts 2:25

Day 74 2 Corinthians 2:14

A Note from the Author

"Prayer changes things," Anna Joy said.

"I believe God is calling me to start an intercessory prayer group. Let's pray as the Lord leads: for individuals, people groups, current events, and nations. The Lord delights in us partnering with him to bring his kingdom on earth as it is in heaven."

Anna Joy's prayers not only changed her but also her relationship with the Lord. The intimate relationship she experienced with him influenced many individuals and groups, crossing cultural and national boundaries.

Every week for over ten years, Anna Joy gathered a small group of prayer warriors to fast and pray. Each week, the Lord guided us in prayer and often imparted inspired messages to us through Anna Joy. I wrote them down as she spoke. They offered us instruction, encouragement, and hope.

I believe these words, inspired by the Lord, were also meant for the body of Christ. With this in mind, I transcribed these messages and compiled them into this ninety-day devotional. After each devotion, you will find a crafted prayer to provide a starting place from which you can add your own prayers. Added Scriptures provide an opportunity for further reflection. May you, too, be encouraged and inspired by the scriptural truths embodied in these devotional words.

Day 1

Draw near to God and He will draw near to you.

James 4:8 (NKJV)

Be still and know that I am God. Do not be afraid of me, my child. I come to you. You have called me, and I draw near. You have drawn near to me, and I am near. I have come, child, as you have asked me to. I am here for you, my child. Just trust me. Let me hold you. Let me draw you near. Come, child, come unto me. Do not pull away but come.

You have come; you have come! You've finally come! Rejoice, child! Rejoice with me, and you will be free. You will be free from pain and free from all sin. You will be washed clean, my child, clean within. No longer will you be bound by what has bound you. I live in you, and you live in me. We are no longer two but one.

You felt as though you walked alone. No more, no more! Do not pull away. Be still. I am not going to hurt you. I am not going to reject you or even rebuke you. I am going to love you and set you free from the fear that has eaten up your life. If you draw near to me, I will draw near to you. Stay with me, abide in my presence, and I will purify you. It is my presence that purifies you.

In the past, you settled for an occasional experience of my presence, an occasional experience of my glory. That is not enough, nor what I planned. Moses came every day to speak with me and be in my presence. In my presence, you will be changed from glory to glory and from strength to strength. You were made in the image of my Son, who died for you. All that binds you will fall away. Nothing evil can stand in my presence. But I have made you able to stand in my presence. Not occasionally, but every day.

Prayer: Lord, I come! Thank you for fully loving and fully accepting me. I rejoice in your invitation to come into your presence. Not a sometimes presence but continually abiding in your love and where I am changed into your image, reflecting your glory.

For Further Reflection:

1 Chronicles 16:10–11
Matthew 11:28–30
2 Corinthians 3:17–18

Day 2

"For I know the plans I have for you," declares the LORD, "plans to prosper you and not to harm you, plans to give you hope and a future."

Jeremiah 29:11 (NIV)

Do not be afraid, my people. There is nothing you will face that I will not help you with. I will cause you to triumph in every place, in every circumstance, and in every situation you face. I am a God who is for you, not against you. My plans and my gifts for you are good things, wonderful things. If you could only know all the good things I think about you and the wonderful plans I made for you. Since they are my plans, they cannot be easily thwarted, especially by you, because I knew you before I made them. You can rest assured that I have plans for you for good and not evil, full of hope and good things.

Will you walk through hard places? Yes. I have told you over and over not to fear evil, for I care for you. There is nothing in your life that I cannot handle. Nothing in your life that I cannot enable you to handle.

There is no reason to fear. Instead, rejoice and find out what kind of God you serve, a God who loves you, and is indeed in you—and for you.

I proved that a long time ago when I sent you my best, my own Son, Jesus, and asked him to die for you. I gave you my best. There is no better that I can give. If you have already seen the best, think about what is coming. There are no bad gifts with me. Do not be afraid, for it is not a matter of good or bad. In my economy, good things grow in bad places. In my economy, all things are possible. Your life doesn't have to be all good or all bad. There will be good things for you in every place you walk. Just remember to look for them and expect them.

Prayer: *Thank you, Father, that your plans for me are good plans, filled with hope. I will not fear the future, for you guide me with your loving care. With a grateful heart, I receive all the good gifts you have for me.*

For Further Reflection:

Isaiah 41:13
Romans 8:31–32
James 1:17

Day 3

For all the promises of God in Him are Yes, and in Him Amen, to the glory of God through us.

2 Corinthians 1:20 (NKJV)

Listen to what you sing. Sing, shout, and praise! Praise, sing, and shout until you experience my presence and my power. Do what you say. Sing, shout, dance, until the power of the Lord comes.

Just as in Joshua's time, the Israelites shouted, and the walls came down. I kept my word to them despite their unfaithfulness. For I am faithful. Every promise to them I kept. I will keep my promises to you if you believe, know, and expect them to come. Look to me, for I have all the promises in my hand. I bring them special delivery so I can see you rejoice and honor me.

Persevere in your waiting. To endure the wait does not mean gritting your teeth, tying a knot, and holding on. It means to rejoice and wait, sing, believe, hope, and be assured that everything I've said to you is coming. Thank me for what I said I will do. Praise me for what I've already done. There is more I haven't yet told you that I will do.

I came that your joy may be full. I will keep my promises. I have not changed, and I will keep my word. Look to me, for I have all the promises in my hand.

Prayer: *Thank you for the promises you have given me because you love me and delight in me. I will rejoice and praise you as I wait for your promises to come to pass. Lord, you only give good gifts to me. You are faithful.*

For Further Reflection:

Psalm 27:13–14
Psalm 47:1–8
Hebrews 10:35–37

Day 4

This is the day the Lord has made; We will rejoice and be glad in it.

Psalm 118:24 (NKJV)

Stop looking for tomorrow. I Am who I Am. And I Am in your today. If you look for me, you will meet me there in your today. You will even find me in the things you hate to do. My hand is on yours, doing those things you dislike doing. You do not do them alone. You will find joy in the most boring, mundane, and disgusting tasks because I am doing them with you.

I will walk you through your days and lead you through your tomorrows. I go with you through the nights, and I walk through your days. None of your days will be wasted. You will find yourself resting in my peace and rejoicing in my Spirit. I am yours, and you are mine.

Prayer: *Thank you, Lord, that you promise me your rest, your peace, and even joy in my most mundane tasks because I am doing them with you. None of my days are wasted, for you walk with me every day.*

For Further Reflection:

Deuteronomy 31:8
Philippians 4:13
Colossians 3:23–24

Day 5

My eyes are always on the Lord, *for he rescues me from the traps of my enemies.*

Psalm 25:15 (NLT)

Do you know how to keep your eyes on me while your physical eyes see what is going on all around you? You see those things, but don't turn your eyes to them. See them but perceive them in your spirit. See what is truly happening, not your circumstances. Keep your eyes on the Lord. Let the eyes of your spirit discern what is happening around you. For only by your spirit can you understand and know me.

Have you learned to daily keep your eyes on me? If not, I will teach you, and I will open the eyes of your spirit. The eyes of the physical man and soulish man need to see me, for they are easily pulled down into despair.

I have strengthened each of my people with might in their spirit man so they will see what is going on around them while looking at me. For no matter what is happening around you, I am greater.

Yes, the corruption of the earth is spreading, and the consequences of sin are worse. But I am greater. I have overcome sin by the blood of the Lamb and by the word of my testimony.

I have sent my Son, and he conquered sin, nailing it to his cross. Sin cannot win, even though it seems to be increasing in strength.

I am the victor, and I make each of you a victor with me. I give each of you a part in my victory. Remember to see with the eyes of the spirit man instead of with the eyes of a carnal and soulish person. Keep your eyes on me.

Prayer: Lord, I will keep my eyes focused on you and not on my circumstances, for you are greater than anything I face. Thank you for opening my spiritual eyes to see you and to discern what is happening around me.

For Further Reflection:

Psalm 16:7–9
2 Corinthians 4:16–18
1 John 5:6–9

Day 6

If I say, "Surely the darkness will hide me and the light become night around me," even the darkness will not be dark to you; the night will shine like the day, for darkness is as light to you.

Psalm 139:11–12 (NIV)

There are no circumstances that belong to the Enemy. Do not fear what Satan can do or has already done. My grace abounds in darkness and abounds in the medium that Satan likes to think is his alone. Everyone and everything is mine. I intend to give you back everything that the Enemy has taken from you and more besides.

When you are in darkness, you cannot see the blessings ahead of you, beside you, or all around you. But I ride on the darkness. The darkness is my chariot that brings me to you.

There will be days when the clouds seem so black they hide the sun completely. But in time, the clouds roll away, and the sun is still there shining brightly. You wonder why you couldn't see it when the sun is so much stronger than any cloud you see. It only seems as though I am not there.

The light is still there in the darkness because I am there, and I am the light. No one stands alone. You stand with me. I am there, and I am the light.

Prayer: *Lord, you are the light that shines brighter than any darkness I may face. Thank you for your continual grace that leads me out of darkness and into the light of your presence, where you enable me to stand with you.*

For Further Reflection:

Psalm 18:28
John 8:12
1 John 1:5

Day 7

"And I tell you that you are Peter, and on this rock I will build my church, and the gates of Hades will not overcome it."

Matthew 16:18 (NIV)

I am preparing a triumphant church, a church that will reign with me in majesty, a church that will reign with me in glory. I am teaching each one in my church to reign with me. Climb the steps of praise despite the winds of circumstances, the winds of doctrine, man's ways, or the devil's ways.

I am preparing a church that will not be blown around but rooted, grounded, and stable in me. A church that will stand in the presence of the Enemy, and nothing shall harm it. A church that will do damage against the kingdom of darkness. The kingdom of darkness may look as though it prevails, but it cannot. My church will stand strong against all that the Enemy brings upon it, and my church shall bring great harm and chaos to the Enemy's kingdom. The Enemy's kingdom will not prevail.

Each one in my church will be a conqueror. I am restoring all that the Enemy has stolen. I am restoring your knowledge of who you are in me, and what I have purposed for you to do. All the knowledge that has been obscured will now bring you up higher to where you should be, where I want you to be with me. No matter what the circumstances are, I want you to live and breathe and have your being with me, never distracted by the things around you. Know that you are more than a conqueror because I love you.

Prayer: Thank you, Lord, that I live, breathe, and have my being in you. I am rooted and grounded in you. Thank you for teaching me how to be more than a conqueror and to reign with you in glory.

For Further Reflection:

Romans 8:37–39
Colossians 2:6–7
Revelation 5:9–10

Day 8

"He who overcomes [the world through believing that Jesus is the Son of God], I will grant to him [the privilege] to sit beside Me on My throne, as I also overcame and sat down beside My Father on His throne."

Revelation 3:21 (AMP)

My people, don't be afraid anymore. Follow me. I will show you where I have meant for you to be. You won't be alone any longer on the earth. You will know that you live in my presence, for you will know that I am your God.

Praise me. Praise me. Come with me. Come up higher. Come where I am. I will show you the throne of the Lamb. You will sit with me. No more fear. No longer afraid. You will rule over all that ruled you. I will rule through you.

***Prayer:** I praise you, Lord, for seating me in heavenly places to rule and reign with you. Thank you that I live safely and securely in your presence.*

For Further Reflection:

Deuteronomy 31:8
Ephesians 2:4–7
Revelation 4:1–11

Day 9

"No one lights a lamp and puts it in a place where it will be hidden, or under a bowl. Instead they put it on its stand, so that those who come in may see the light."

Luke 11:33 (NIV)

The world is indeed growing darker, and the sin around you is more pronounced. But where sin abounds, grace abounds even more. Grace is more available now because of the sin that is growing stronger. But this grace must be asked for, must be appropriated, must be treasured, and must be used in order to be effective.

In the same way, as darkness grows, so does the power of light in you. It grows brighter and brighter within you as the darkness grows around you. If you are looking to blend in and hide, don't try, for you will only be miserable. You cannot hide the light. As the darkness grows, even the dimmest light will be light. Not that your light should be dim but brightly shining.

Seek my face. Seek my help. Seek the oil you need to keep your lamps bright and glowing, for you are going to need the power of my Spirit. Live by my sight. The oil is a symbol of the power of the Holy Spirit. Only lamps bright and clear hold light. I am the light of the world, and I am in you. Do not be afraid to let the light shine or be afraid of the consequences, for the reward of bearing this light is eternal.

Prayer: I thank you for your grace, your enabling presence, to be a light in this world. Thank you for giving me your Holy Spirit to help me and guide me as I seek your face.

For Further Reflection:

Proverbs 4:18
John 8:12
Romans 5:20–21

Day 10

You, Lord, keep my lamp burning; my God turns my darkness into light.

Psalm 18:28 (NIV)

Lift me higher and higher in everything you do. Lift me higher in your words and actions, in everyday living. Let others see that I am in your life. I made you different—bright and shining in a difficult world. To have joy when there is no reason to have joy.

Do not look at the circumstances or the darkness around you. Draw near to me. Draw near to me when you feel most afraid or most depressed. Let me wash you clean. Let me keep your light shining bright by my might and power.

Prayer: *Thank you, Lord, that you have cleansed me and called me out of darkness into the light of your presence. I will exalt your name no matter what circumstances I face. When there seems to be no reason for me to be joyful, you fill my heart with your joy.*

For Further Reflection:

1 Chronicles 29:10–13
Psalm 42:11
John 12:32

Day 11

"You will seek me and find me when you seek me with all your heart."

Jeremiah 29:13 (NIV)

Seek me with all your heart and soul. Seek me with all that is within you. Give nothing to the world that would hold you back. When you seek me with all your heart, I will be there to be found by you. I promise you that I will come to you. You will know me, and I shall know you. We will walk together in love. You will know my heart. You will know my mind, and all that I am doing.

When you see all that I have done, and when you see all that I am doing, run and join me. Allow me to work through you. Don't be afraid. Seek my face as we walk together in love.

Prayer: Lord, I seek your face. I am excited about getting to know you and joining you in what you are doing. Thank you for sharing your thoughts with me and revealing your heart as we walk together in love.

For Further Reflection:

Psalm 27:4
Psalm 105:3–4
Ephesians 2:8–10

Day 12

"Very truly I tell you, the Son can do nothing by himself; he can do only what he sees his Father doing, because whatever the Father does the Son also does."

John 5:19 (NIV)

In the past, you have come to me and told me what you are doing. Now, I am seeking people to come to me and listen for me to tell them what I am doing and what I would like to do. In the past, I have asked you to let me into your world to share with me what you are doing. Now, I am giving you an invitation to come into my life, as I have come into yours, and let you share in what I am doing.

I want you to do things with me. I want you to do what my Son did. I want you to do what I am doing. I want you to do what I am doing with me. I want to do it through you. Won't you come into my world and let me do things through you, as I have come into your world to do things with you?

I want you to bring light to my world, to do what I am doing. Will you join me? I need many people to reach all my people.

Prayer: Lord, I come to you with a listening heart. Thank you for wanting to reveal to me what you are doing so I can join you in accomplishing the work you have planned.

For Further Reflection:

Jeremiah 33:3
John 14:12–14
Revelation 3:20–22

Day 13

When Peter saw him, he asked,
"Lord, what about him?"
Jesus answered, "If I want him to
remain alive until I return, what is
that to you? You must follow me."

John 21:21–22 (NIV)

I need people to be willing to do what I have called them to do. Some I have asked to pray. Others I tell to go. Some I called to speak. Others I will tell to teach. I need people who will do what I say and no longer look around to see what I am doing with another. People who would be faithful to do what I ask them to do.

I asked Peter to tend my lambs, feed my sheep. He asked about John. I told him that it was not his business what I do with another person.

The key is to do what I ask. I promise you that you will be a harvester of souls around the world.

Prayer: *Lord, I focus my eyes on you and not on what you are doing with those around me. Thank you for creating a purpose and calling unique for me so I may have a part in leading others to you.*

For Further Reflection:

John 4:34–38
John 21:15–23
Romans 12:3–8

Day 14

"'Not by might nor by power, but by my Spirit,' says the Lord of hosts. 'Who are you, O great mountain? Before Zerubbabel you shall become a plain! And he shall bring forth the capstone with shouts of "Grace, grace to it!"'"

Zechariah 4:6–7 (NKJV)

In the coming weeks, remember the words that I have spoken to you—not by might, not by power, but by my Spirit. When the mountain looms large, remember to speak my grace to it, for you will see the mountain moved. Climb the steps of praise that lead into my presence. I am as close to you as the word that is in your mouth.

Sometimes people ask how they can make my presence real. They make it so hard when it is so easy. Simply believe what the Word says. I am as close to you as the word in your mouth. When you speak that word of praise, of thanksgiving, it brings you into my presence, into the courts, into the gates, and into my presence.

It is not hard. It may be difficult, but when it is, speak my grace to the mountain. Jesus will become the cornerstone. The mountain will be moved out of your way. Nothing will block your access to me if you want my presence.

Prayer: *Lord, when troubles seem to overshadow me like mountains, I will enter your presence with praise and thanksgiving. You are the answer to every problem. My praise opens the eyes of my heart to hear your voice.*

For Further Reflection:

Deuteronomy 30:11–14
Psalm 100:1–5
Mark 11:22–24

Day 15

The Lord will extend your mighty scepter from Zion, saying, "Rule in the midst of your enemies!"

Psalm 110:2 (NIV)

Remember what I have told you before. There will be mountains to face. Some of my people have come face-to-face with mountains this week, but grace is the answer. Grace abounds where sin abounds. Grace abounds more than sin. Be thankful for the darkness, for there is more grace. Grace is the weapon with the power of my Spirit behind it.

My people have nothing to fear. They will triumph in the midst of my enemies. The Enemy will be forced to watch while you celebrate my victory over him. Remember what Scripture says: you are to reign in the presence of your enemies. Not that you must hide from them. But rule and reign in their presence. No longer shall they rule and reign over my people. I break the bonds from off my people, and my people shall rule and reign.

Do not fear the darkness around you or the Enemy that hides there. I am the Lord of the darkness. It is my chariot. The Enemy uses the darkness to hide in, but I use it to ride on. You will rule and reign. Now is the time to learn to do just that.

Prayer: *Lord, your grace causes me to triumph over every mountain, every obstacle, every problem. I have no reason to fear. Thank you for teaching me how to rule and reign over the Enemy through the power of the Holy Spirit.*

For Further Reflection:

Psalm 18:6–19
Romans 5:20–21
2 Corinthians 9:8

Day 16

Casting all your care upon Him,
for He cares for you.

1 Peter 5:7 (NKJV)

My people, my little ones, my own dear ones that I love so much. How I wish to relieve you from the strain and stress you feel from the responsibility of carrying so much. I want to carry your present, and so many of you are carrying the cares of the past with the present as well as the fears of the future. You are not equipped to carry the cares of your present alone, much less the cares of the past and the fears of the future. You are not equipped.

I want to relieve my church from carrying the cares of the past, the present, and the fears of the future. I want to shoulder this burden. I want to deliver you from the bondage of responsibility that is not true responsibility. Yes, I call you to be responsible servants, but not to carry what is not yours to carry. I will deliver you from those burdens under which so many labor and are sick and die.

I will deliver you, heal, and restore you, for this is what I wish for each one of my precious servants.

Prayer: Lord, I give you all my concerns. I give you all the things that you never meant for me to carry. I know you will take care of everything I place in your hands. I rejoice in your gift of rest designed to free me from burden or weariness.

For Further Reflection:

Psalm 55:22
Matthew 11:28–30
Philippians 4:6–7

Day 17

For through him we both have access
to the Father by one Spirit.

Ephesians 2:18 (NIV)

Don't you understand that you always live in my presence? When you accepted my Son as Lord and Savior, I came to live in you. You now live in me. We are one. We have always been together. My people do not understand. You always live in my presence. There is no barrier between you and me. My Son bought your access to me through my Spirit, in his name and through his blood. You don't have to wait until you die. You already have access to me and access to my Spirit. My Spirit shows you the way to go. Let him teach you, for you know him deep down in your spirit. Let him flow into every cell of your being.

My church is a part of me, not being made one, but we *are* one. You were inside of me when you were baptized into his death. You were raised inside my kingdom. Praise and worship are the language of my kingdom and bring you into my presence, so you are able to speak to me and understand as I speak to you. The Enemy says that you must wait until tomorrow before I give you access. You had access to me the moment you were washed in my Son's blood.

Prayer: I praise you, Lord, that by your blood shed on the cross, you removed every barrier that would separate us. By your Spirit, I always have access to you and your presence.

For Further Reflection:

Romans 5:1–2
Colossians 1:19–22
Hebrews 10:19–23

Day 18

"Now my soul is troubled, and what shall I say? 'Father, save me from this hour'? No, it was for this very reason I came to this hour. Father, glorify your name!" Then a voice came from heaven, "I have glorified it, and will glorify it again."

John 12:27–28 (NIV)

My Son said to me, "Glorify your name," just before the worst trial in his life.

I responded, "I have glorified you, and I will glorify you again."

I have glorified myself in each of your lives, and I will do it again. I will be glorified in my church. In the believer's life, I am the Lord. As my Son experienced, often my glory comes in the worst situations. Don't run from those situations, but come to me, and let me take you through those situations and use them to bring glory to my name.

Prayer: *Lord, when troubles come, I will still myself in you and allow you to take me through those situations. Thank you for using the trials in my life as a testimony of what you did for me and how you helped me overcome, because your new nature lives in me.*

For Further Reflection:

Romans 8:16–18
Ephesians 3:20–21
Colossians 3:1–4

Day 19

You make known to me the path of life; you will fill me with joy in your presence, with eternal pleasures at your right hand.

Psalm 16:11 (NIV)

I said in my Word that in my presence, you would be changed from glory to glory, strength to strength, faith to faith, and grace to grace. Why do you hesitate to come into my presence, to place yourself in my presence every day and every minute? You can walk in my presence. Why do you hesitate? Most of my people believe that I spend their whole lifetime changing them to be more like me. This is true, but I also want you to know me.

The capacity to know me has already been given to you if you bring yourself into my presence. If you come to me and sit with me, even while doing other things, you will come to know me. You will spend a lifetime filled with happiness, filled with joy, and filled with blessedness. You will know that you are my child, my creation.

I chose to make you. I chose to redeem you. I chose to give my life for you. Why does it take a lifetime to approach me when I have opened wide the doors? Why don't you come to know me and spend a lifetime together? You have the notion that you must do other things first, or you must spend time with me first so you can do other things. Put me first but see that I am with you in all things. You don't go to work without me. You don't go to school without me. You don't go anywhere without me. You don't take a breath without me. I am always there, standing beside you, waiting for you to acknowledge my presence, a presence felt by you.

Prayer: Lord, thank you that you delight in me as your much-loved child. You have given me the capacity to know you and experience the joy of your presence. You are always with me. You desire to be with me in everything I do.

For Further Reflection:

Acts 17:24–28
2 Corinthians 3:18
Ephesians 1:3–6

Day 20

"On that day you will realize that I am in my Father, and you are in me, and I am in you."

John 14:20 (NIV)

You make our oneness so hard when it is so easy. It amounts to saying, "Lord, I am here," with the knowledge that my answer is, "I am here too." We are one. We are no longer separate but one. You live in me as well as I live in you. We are no longer separate.

I promise if you come to me, you will see me as Moses did, as Samuel did, and many others besides them. It is not for some glad day after a while or when you die. It is for today. I wish to do things with you, even the mundane things, but the way to make them holy is to do them with me. And let me do them with you.

***Prayer**: Lord, thank you for delighting in doing all things with me, including mundane tasks. I delight in our oneness—I in you, and you in me.*

For Further Reflection:

1 Corinthians 6:17
John 17:20–24
Philippians 2:13

Day 21

Christ loved the church and gave himself up for her to make her holy, cleansing her by the washing with water through the word, and to present her to himself as a radiant church, without stain or wrinkle or any other blemish, but holy and blameless.

Ephesians 5:25–27 (NIV)

You say to me, "I can't come to you. It's as if I'm naked. I'm sinful, warped, twisted, crooked."

I forgive you. I forgave you when you first came to me. I forgave all your sins. I even began to straighten out the consequences of your sins. Yes, your old nature was crooked, twisted, gnarled, and deformed. But I have given you a new nature in Christ.

I will wash the spots, straighten the crooked, and heal the wounded. I am a perfect God, and I will have a bride without spot or wrinkle.

If you sit in my presence, I promise I will straighten the twisted and crooked places, iron out the wrinkles, and bleach out the spots. There will be no blemish in my beloved bride. No blemish at all. In my eyes, it is already done, so let it be done in your eyes, for I tell you it is so. Will you agree with me?

Prayer: *Thank you, Lord, that you have forgiven me completely, cleansed me, and given me your new nature in Christ. Thank you that I am perfect in your eyes—your beloved bride, without spot or blemish.*

For Further Reflection:

2 Corinthians 5:17
Ephesians 4:21–24
Revelation 19:7–9

Day 22

Serve one another in love.

Galatians 5:13 (NLT)

Don't you see, children? Love in action is servanthood. It is not slavery. Jesus was and is my Son. Not my slave. But because he obeyed me, he became your servant, while he was yet God, even to the point of laying down his life. He didn't do it because I ordered him to do it. But he wanted to because he loves you and wants to unite us again. Satan has always sought to divide us, you and me.

Obedience is not slavery, but it is choosing to do as I ask because you love me. It is choosing to serve your fellow man because I love them, and I want you to love them too. It is not slavery or a list of rules. It is the fruit of the heart. Obedience is the fruit of love. Nothing brings you joy like doing something for the sake of someone you love.

As co-laborers, you and I together usher new Christians, new believers, into my kingdom. There is nothing like watching a new baby being born or learning to walk. Watching the discovery and joy on their faces makes the days serving them worth it, no matter how hard it seems.

I am giving the joy of discovery back to my church because it has been lost. Because of this loss, my people have had no power, enthusiasm, or the ability to show forth my presence, even though my presence is there. It is the joy of discovery, of finding something new in me, something new in your life, something new for you to do. This is a joy that gives you vision for the future and a hope for tomorrow that is for good and not for evil.

Prayer: Thank you, Lord, that you want to take me on a journey of discovery as I serve you by serving others. You will also give me a new vision filled with hope and delight for my future as I co-labor with you.

For Further Reflection:

Luke 22:24–27
John 15:9–17
Galatians 4:4–7

Day 23

He lifted me out of the slimy pit, out of the mud and mire; he set my feet on a rock and gave me a firm place to stand. He put a new song in my mouth, a hymn of praise to our God.

Psalm 40:2–3 (NIV)

I know, my people, that there are many of you who are mired in the pit. The way out of the pit is the song that I put in your mouth in the darkest circumstances. I can and do give you a song. My favorite time to give you a song is in the darkest circumstances of your life. That song will lift you and others out of the miry pit and place your feet upon Jesus, the rock that lasts. Your enemies shall be under your feet.

Many of you have found yourself in a pit because you obeyed me, and by obeying me, you landed in the pit. You thought you heard me wrong, or that I deserted you, but that is not true. I put a song in you that is a ladder to pull you out of the pit. A song that will pull others out of the same pit you were in. You think that you have to manufacture praise and come up with a song, but you don't. If you look to me and call to me for help, I will put a song in your mouth. I will show you a vision of my majesty that will cause a song to bubble up out of you and out of many others.

If you hadn't been in the pit, you wouldn't have known that I would lift you out of the pit and lift others out too. It was not a mistake but part of my plan. Everything that is in your life has been molded to the plan that I have for each one of you. There is nothing that does not turn out for good or is not molded into my plan for your life. Do not worry. You will not be left behind.

Prayer: Lord, thank you that you give me your song in the night—a song to sing in my darkest places—a song that will lift me out of the pit of despair. Thank you, Lord. I trust you to work all my circumstances together for good, even when I don't understand how that can be possible.

For Further Reflection:

Psalm 42:8–11
Romans 8:28
Colossians 3:15–17

Day 24

"But you will receive power when the Holy Spirit comes on you; and you will be my witnesses in Jerusalem, and in all Judea and Samaria, and to the ends of the earth."

Acts 1:8 (NIV)

I want you to be witnesses for me, to lift me up high so that others will see me. I am calling all of my church to be a witness for me. I am preparing experiences with me that will enable you to witness to others in the world around you. You cannot be a witness to what you have not known or experienced. The reason many in my church are reluctant to witness is that they have not experienced my presence and my power in such a way that they cannot help but speak of me.

I am preparing a deluge of my presence and power to fall on each person in my church. I will come to each one from the oldest to the youngest, and not one will be left behind. You will be delivered from all that bound you, and you will bring deliverance to others. You will lift me high and not exalt your experiences. But you will exalt me and say that I can do far more than what I have already done for you.

I am telling each of you that you will be my witnesses in your city, in your state, in your country, and around the world. You will be my witnesses as my disciples were so long ago.

Prayer: Thank you, Lord, for the power of your Spirit that delivers me out of bondage. May I be a witness of your power and help lead others out of bondage and into the freedom of our new nature in Christ.

For Further Reflection:

Isaiah 43:10–12
Matthew 28:18–20
Ephesians 3:20–21

Day 25

"Therefore everyone who hears these words of mine and puts them into practice is like a wise man who built his house on the rock. The rain came down, the streams rose, and the winds blew and beat against that house; yet it did not fall, because it had its foundation on the rock."

Matthew 7:24–25 (NIV)

Build your house upon the rock. I didn't say there would not be storms. I promised there would be storms, even fierce storms. But the storms that are coming will not remove you from the rock on which you have built your life. They will not overflow or overcome you. I am the rock on which you stand firm.

I promised all my children a kingdom. You will receive the keys of the kingdom and knowledge of how to use them. You will find that nothing the Enemy does can overcome the kingdom of God, whether storm, trial, or tribulation. The Enemy thinks that he is in control. But

I am. I permit his work for a time, but it will not bring about what he plans to accomplish.

Stand on the rock. My Son will make you stand. Do not worry. I know that you sometimes feel weak, frail, and unfaithful. But that is not the truth. My Son died for you. No devil shall stop you. You shall come through without a stain. You are washed clean. Stand firm, knowing the truth.

Prayer: *Thank you, Lord, that I will not be overcome by my trials or by the Enemy because I stand on your promises even when my circumstances oppose the truth of your Word. You will cause me to stand firm in you.*

For Further Reflection:

Psalm 18:1–3
Psalm 27:5–6
Psalm 62:5–8

Day 26

For God has not given us a spirit of fear, but of power and of love and of a sound mind.

2 Timothy 1:7 (NKJV)

Do not be afraid. Do not be frightened. My presence has banished fear, for perfect love casts out all fear. I am perfect love. I have not given you a spirit of fear, but a spirit of power, love, and a sound mind. I have not given you a spirit of fear, leading you back into bondage, but a spirit by which you cry out, "Abba, Father!"

When you cry out to me, I will help you. I will sustain you. I will uphold you. Do not be afraid. Do not let yourself fear, for I am with you all the days of your life. I am with all who call upon my name. I will uphold you with my own strength and power. I will be there for you. You can depend on me.

Prayer: *Lord, your overwhelming love for me drives out all fear. Therefore, I am not afraid. I am safe and secure in your presence.*

For Further Reflection:

Isaiah 41:10
Romans 8:14–16
1 John 4:16–19

Day 27

"This is what the Lord says to you: 'Do not be afraid or discouraged because of this vast army. For the battle is not yours, but God's.'"

2 Chronicles 20:15 (NIV)

I have called you to face fear, but not alone. I am the great Shepherd. I told the Israelites to face the giants. I did not say there would be no giants, but that I would be with them and go before them to bring the giants down.

I want to be your God, to bring you a testimony that you can shout from the housetops, a testimony that brings you great joy. This is an opportunity. It is not a battle that you can lose if you let me fight it. However, the battle is not between you and the Enemy but between the Enemy and me. I have already defeated him. And I defeat him in your life. I also protect you from him. You will know me as a personal God, as someone who fights for you. Your joy will be full.

Do not be afraid to face the giants. Just remember who the grasshoppers are. They are not you. Remember who they face, for I am a mighty God.

Prayer: Thank you, Lord, that you fight for me. You have already gone before me and won every battle. You will enable me to overcome any adversity. Then I will be able to shout your victory with joy.

For Further Reflection:

Exodus 15:6
Psalm 91:1–16
Ephesians 6:10–18

Day 28

Oh, clap your hands, all you peoples! Shout to God with the voice of triumph! For the LORD Most High is awesome; He is a great King over all the earth.

Psalm 47:1–2 (NKJV)

Do not lose your song in the presence of the giants. Sing through the battle. Do not lose the song I have given you to sing as you march through the battle. Sing forth your praises. Sing forth the song I have put in you. Shout until you see the power of the Lord.

Shout because I fight for you. Shout because the giants are going to fall. Shout because I am the problem solver. Shout because I have put a song in your heart and mind. Shout because you are not the grasshopper. The giants are only in front of you, as well as the mountains, which shall become molehills. The giants in front of you are only illusions. They are demonic, a screen, an illusion of fear to keep you from going through them. Remember, you are going through. Beyond this passage is a place filled with my promises and healing.

***Prayer**: Thank you, Lord, for placing shouts of joy and songs of praise in my heart. Help me remember to sing and praise you through every trial, for you are faithful.*

For Further Reflection:

Psalm 5:11–12
Psalm 66:1–5
Acts 16:25–26

Day 29

"Have I not commanded you? Be strong and courageous. Do not be afraid; do not be discouraged, for the LORD your God will be with you wherever you go."

Joshua 1:9 (NIV)

Do not walk in fear, my child. I am always near you. Fear is not my gift to you. Fear belongs to the Evil One, not to God's beloved Son. The Son now lives and loves in you. Fear must not live in you. When you see fear coming, run to me quickly, my child. Let me hold you. Fear shall not live in my own. You live within me.

Fear no longer lives in you. You are mine. I am yours forever. I will stay with you, my child, as you walk along my way. Yes, child, I love you. I love you, my precious one.

Prayer: Thank you, Lord, that I am precious to you and you love me completely. You never leave me to fight a battle alone. Fear has no place in me because your love fills me until there is no room for fear.

For Further Reflection:

Jeremiah 31:3
1 John 3:1–2
1 John 4:16–19

Day 30

"Whoever believes will not act hastily."

Isaiah 28:16 (NKJV)

The feeling of being overwhelmed can cause you to make decisions in a hurry. Those who believe in me do not make hasty decisions. Be at rest, be quiet, and wait. All that needs to get done will be done. You may feel that everything must be done right now. When you hear, "Hurry up," that is the time to wait.

If you believe in me, you will wait on me. Those who believe in me do not make haste. They wait for me. Those who believe in the Father and in me will wait for me. I will do all the things you need me to do.

Do not worry. All things that need to be done will be done. They will be done by the power of my Spirit and not by your own might and power. All who believe in faith shall find this power. Learn to wait. Do not make haste. Those who believe in me do not make haste.

***Prayer**: Lord, you invite me to rest in you and trust in your help. I choose to wait in your presence and listen for direction from your Holy Spirit when I am pressured to make hasty decisions.*

For Further Reflection:

Psalm 27:13–14
Isaiah 40:28–31
Matthew 11:28–30

Day 31

"I in them and you in me—so that they may be brought to complete unity. Then the world will know that you sent me and have loved them even as you have loved me."

John 17:23 (NIV)

It is indeed true that I, Jesus, prayed for my Father to unite you so the world would know he sent me. There is another reason for that unity—so they might know that my Father loves you as he loves me.

The world won't know this until they see my people working and flowing together as one. Then they will know I, the Father, love them as I loved my Son and sent him to become a man and die for them. I love each one of you that much. The only way the world will believe I sent my Son is if my church unites as one and my Spirit flows through my people, as he flowed through my Son. For this unity, you need my Spirit of might.

Even now, even today, the melding and the smelting of my body together as one is coming to pass and will continue. There will come a day when people will malign you. But they will not find anything of which to accuse you. The charges they bring against you will be as false as the charges against my Son. When you walk in love, you will not break any of my commandments. And they will see that I'm a God of love. They will repent of their unbelief. And so will you.

Prayer: Lord, you loved us so much that you sent your beloved Son to die for us. May your Spirit flow in our lives, uniting us in your love so that others will believe in you and your Son, Jesus.

For Further Reflection:

Psalm 133:1–3
Ephesians 4:1–6
Philippians 2:1–4

Day 32

The blood of Jesus Christ His Son
cleanses us from all sin.

1 John 1:7 (NKJV)

Once, long ago, I washed the feet of my disciples. I told them that those who bathe are clean and only need to wash their feet.[1] My blood cleanses you. Nothing can stand between us when you avail yourself of my blood. You will walk in my presence and receive all you need. There is no interval, no time span, but only my blood.

Prayer: *Lord, thank you for your precious blood shed for us on the cross. Thank you that your blood cleanses us and knows no bounds.*

---

1 John 13

For Further Reflection:

Ephesians 1:3–14
Hebrews 9:11–15
1 Peter 1:17–21

Day 33

Surely you have granted him unending blessings and made him glad with the joy of your presence.

Psalm 21:6 (NIV)

I want you to serve me with joy and gladness. Yes, you will have tribulations. Yes, you will have trials. Yes, you will have hard places. But you will walk with me in my presence. You will walk with joy in your hearts, and the strength that this joy gives you will be yours.

Yes, you will face new things, things you were sure you could not overcome. But I will be there. I have overcome the world. I am the overcomer, and I make you an overcomer.

I want you to serve me with joy. You will experience suffering, but you will have joy. You suppose that during these times my presence is not with you, but my presence goes with you wherever you go. You will serve me with gladness and joy, much to the consternation of the Enemy.

It is your joy and gladness in hard places that is a witness of me to the unbelievers.

No matter how hard the circumstances are in your life, my final words to you will be, "Well done, my good and faithful servant. Enter into the presence of the Lord with joy. Enter into my eternal presence." You never have to fight to make it into my presence. Know that you are in my presence. This is what heaven is—rejoicing in the presence of God. I designed eternal life to start here on earth, in my presence.

Draw strength as you praise me, for in your praises you will find that my presence wraps itself around you like a protective blanket, strengthening and healing you. I want you whole. I want you to be free, glad, and full of joy.

Prayer: Thank you, Lord, that you enable me to rejoice even when I face difficult circumstances. I know you love me and will never leave me alone. The joy of your presence protects me, strengthens me, and frees me. I praise you!

For Further Reflection:

Psalm 16:11
Psalm 84:4–7
1 John 5:4–5

Day 34

My brethren, count it all joy when you fall into various trials, knowing that the testing of your faith produces patience. But let patience have its perfect work, that you may be perfect and complete, lacking nothing.

James 1:2–4 (NKJV)

Count it all joy when trials come to you. I have allowed the trials of your faith so you might come forth as gold. When they are over, you will lack no good thing. Let the trials work patience in your soul. Patience mixed with joy gives equal triumph in the Lord. Let patience have her perfect work so you lack no good thing. Mix patience with the joy I give, and you will triumph.

Your faith grows stronger every day. It grows each day as you pray. You will come forth as pure gold and lack no good thing. Mix my joy with patience, and the victory will surely come to you. Stand still and know that I am God. I will fight for you. Let me fight your battle. I will bring you straight through. Take your place in me. I will bring you victory, and you will sing and shout my praise.

Prayer: *Lord, teach me to trust you when I am in the middle of a trial. Your timing is perfect—never early, never late. I am confident of your love for me. Therefore, I have hope. Even in seasons of waiting, your joy is always available to me. You will cause me to triumph and shout your praises.*

For Further Reflection:

Romans 12:10–12
2 Corinthians 2:14
1 Peter 1:3–8

Day 35

"'I will make a difference between
My people and your people.'"

Exodus 8:23 (NKJV)

I will make a difference between you and those around you so they might ask you who is making the difference or what is making the difference.

You can say, "Without Jesus, I would be nothing. Without Jesus, I would be a failure. Without Jesus, I would be a mess. Jesus lifts me out of my messes. Jesus lifts me out of my failures. Jesus is the reason I can rejoice in situations that once destroyed me and destroyed those around me. Jesus is the reason for my joy."

Prayer: *Thank you, Jesus, that I can rejoice in those situations that once devastated me, because you redeemed my past. Instead of sorrow, you give me joy.*

For Further Reflection:

Isaiah 61:1–4
2 Corinthians 5:17–21
Philippians 3:7–11

Day 36

"Whoever believes in me, as the Scripture has said, 'Out of his heart will flow rivers of living water.'"

John 7:38 (ESV)

So many of my people are like a dry riverbed, having seen no water for a long time. It seems unlikely, and even impossible, that water will ever flow again. I say to my church, you are my church. I say to my schools, you are my schools. I say to the lands, you are my lands. I say to creation, you are my creation. And I am your Lord.

I will reclaim that which is mine. Living water will fill cracked riverbeds and dry deserts in decimated lands that have not seen water for a long time. Water will flow. I claim what my Father dedicated to me in the first place, because I died for all men.

You will again see my strength in your lives and my presence in your churches, schools, homes, and places of employment. My name will be proclaimed throughout your land. I am Lord and always will be. I am Lord, whether you acknowledge me or not. When you acknowledge my lordship, it is a time of pleasant things in the land, and you will be happy. When you do not acknowledge me as Lord, it is a time of trial and pain. It appears I am not there, but I am. I will make deserts fertile land and bring life-giving water.

Already, my people can feel it. They are sensing a difference in themselves. New hope and new expectations are springing up. There shall again be singing in your land because of the God whom you serve.

Prayer: Thank you, Lord, that you are the living water flowing in us and through us, refreshing us and filling all the dry places. You renew our hope and the expectation of good things to come because of your presence in our lives.

For Further Reflection:

Psalm 2:6–8
Isaiah 35:1–10
Isaiah 41:17–20

Day 37

In all these things we are more than conquerors through him who loved us.

Romans 8:37 (NIV)

Lift your heart unto me. Do not be pulled down by the circumstances around you or listen to voices that bring defeat and depression. This is a time of war, not a time of peace. I give you peace in the midst of war. Follow him who leads: my own dear Son.

Do not fear defeat. You have already won. I have given you the victory through righteousness, not defeat. You are not under the Enemy's feet. He is under your feet. Do not let him bring your thoughts, eyes, and understanding away from me and down to your circumstances.

Defend yourself against depression and discouragement by lifting your voice in praise and song. My joy within you is your strength. I have given you power to win every battle.

Prayer: *Lord, sometimes the battle is in my thoughts. Instead of allowing my mind to be overrun by negative thoughts, I will praise and worship you so my thoughts are focused on your majesty instead of on my circumstances.*

For Further Reflection:

Psalm 118:14–16
Isaiah 41:10–13
2 Corinthians 10:3–5

Day 38

For every house is built by someone, but
God is the builder of everything.

Hebrews 3:4 (NIV)

I am the wise master builder. I am in the process of building a city, preparing a city for you. I am building each of you a mansion filled with good things, wonderful things. On earth I am remodeling, building on earth as it is in heaven. On earth, I am remodeling. In heaven, I am building. When I remodel on earth, it looks like I am building new buildings, for sometimes I tear down and destroy before I exalt and raise up. I humble before I exalt.

I guarantee that in both places, my buildings for you will be finished, and my glory shall fill you. I love you more than you could love me. Even your love for me reflects the love I have for you. My building projects shall be finished on earth as well as in heaven.

The work of my hands and the plans of my heart shall be accomplished in your lives, beautiful beyond description. I meant for your time on earth to be a shadow of heaven, with joy unstoppable and indestructible. That joy is not just for heaven, but also for now. I want you to walk with me now. I will not be any different in heaven.

Prayer: Lord, you are the master builder. Sometimes you remove things from my life that are no longer useful or do not reflect your nature. But you only cut away to rebuild. You are the God of restoration. You restore my hope, my strength, and my dreams. Thank you for being the architect of my life—creating your beauty in me and filling me with joy.

For Further Reflection:

John 14:1–3
1 Corinthians 3:9–11
2 Timothy 2:20–21

Day 39

May he strengthen your hearts so that
you will be blameless and holy.

1 Thessalonians 3:13 (NIV)

Your true strength lies in purity and holiness. Your true strength lies in drawing close to me, for I am holy. Without me, you can do nothing. With me, you can do all things, for I strengthen you. Your true strength comes from my purity and holiness flowing in, around, and through you. It comes from the time you spend in my presence and the ways you allow me to fashion you into my image.

Seek me for that purity. Seek me for my holiness, for no man on earth possesses my holiness. No man can give holiness. Only I can keep you pure. You are not able on your own to keep yourself unspotted from the world. As my Son cleansed his disciples by washing their feet, only I can wash you and keep you from the dirt you collect while you are walking through the world. You are walking through the world with me.

Resist the temptation to become distracted and turn aside to the world. Keep yourself focused on me, your destination. Focus on me, your Lord. Focus on me, your God.

I have put you here as a light in the darkness in a world I created and love. I have kept you here because the world needs your light. I am the source of light. You need me for that source. I am the source of holiness and purity. I am the source of your strength. Allow yourself to be drawn to me. Allow yourself to remain in me. There is no place that we will not go together, but there are lots of things we will not do because they soil your garments and weaken your strength. As you go back into the world, I will walk with you and cover you completely.

I call you to holiness so you can funnel strength to the weakest in the world, those who need me the most. I send each one of my people to rescue those who do not know me, those who cannot protect themselves, those who are without hope. I call each person back to me. Let me heal them, hold them, and take care of them.

Prayer: *Lord, I draw near to you, turning my eyes away from the things of the world. As I walk in your holiness, you strengthen me, enabling me to bring that strength and help to those most in need of your hope.*

For Further Reflection:

John 15:1–5
Ephesians 5:8–14
1 Peter 1:13–16

Day 40

"I have told you these things, so that in me you may have peace. In this world you will have trouble. But take heart! I have overcome the world."

John 16:33 (NIV)

I have given you a peace the world cannot destroy and a joy the world cannot take away. Find your peace in me, your joy in me. Stand in my peace and demonstrate my peace to the world. I have told you there would be tribulations and rumors of war. I have told you such things have to be. But in the middle of this, stand in my peace with fullness of joy and hope, looking to me as the author and finisher of your faith.

I am not just the finisher of your faith, but also the finisher of all things in my kingdom. I will leave nothing undone of what I said I would do.

I said in Hebrews that there would be a shaking of everything that could be shaken. I said to you that you serve a kingdom that cannot be shaken. Stand with peace and joy in a hope bent on seeing me. Determine in your heart to come after me. Trust me. Your whole world is a tiny ball in my hands, and I am able to keep it from flying apart.

The key to realizing that your stability and peace are intact is to realize I hold you in the palm of my hand. Your firm ground is in me, and not in the world you walk through. When you feel the ground shifting under you, changing all around you, and you begin to fear, run to me and cry, "Abba, Father!" For I have given you a spirit of adoption and not fear. Let the first hint of tremors send you running to me. In me, you will find stability and safety.

Prayer: Thank you, Lord, that my peace is in you, no matter what is happening around me. I will not fear but, instead, run to you, for you are my safe place. You will hold me secure in your love. In your presence is fullness of joy.

For Further Reflection:

Psalm 46:1–11
Romans 8:14–25
Hebrews 12:26–28

Day 41

Do not be overcome by evil, but
overcome evil with good.

Romans 12:21 (NIV)

Seek not only your good and the good of your country. Instead, seek the God who made you to seek good. Seek the good of your enemies. I sent my Son to die for them, too, and redeem them by his blood. Seek the good of those who don't know him yet. Seek me and my good, not only your good.

In doing so, you will overcome evil with good and show kindness where cruelty prevailed. Grace will flow, and the scars around the world will heal. Love overcomes evil. Then the people will look up and rejoice and say, "Surely there is no one able to do this."

Then you will be able to proclaim the name of my Son, Jesus. When he is lifted up, he will draw all people to himself, even those who were once called your enemies.

Prayer: *Thank you, Lord, for teaching me how to overcome evil with good. May I offer your goodness to those who are unkind to me, to those who don't know you yet, and to those who are hurting so they experience your healing love and rejoice in you.*

For Further Reflection:

Matthew 5:44–48
John 3:14–17
Philippians 2:1–4

Day 42

Furthermore, because we are united with Christ, we have received an inheritance from God, for he chose us in advance, and he makes everything work out according to his plan.

Ephesians 1:11 (NLT)

I have placed each one of my children on earth for a purpose. No one can do what another has been assigned to do or take another's place. Rise up and claim the land I put before you. As you walk with me, you take back the land the Enemy has stolen from you and me. You walk in my victory. Proclaim my name, my lordship, wherever you go. Proclaim it with actions, with love, with confidence, and with peace instead of fear.

Do not be afraid of the opposition, for I can bring them down with a "stone" in your hand, just as I did for David. I am asking for your hand. I will provide the stone and direct it in your hand to bring the Enemy down. I will not forsake you. I want to walk with you even more than you want to walk with me. I love you. I want us to walk together and in agreement. I want to answer your prayers. I made this world for you, but more than that, I made you for me.

There is nothing to fear. You can take the land. Just rise up and be willing to do it. Rise up and trust me to work through you. I want you to have the answer to your prayers and the joy it will bring. So, rise up and take your land. Rise up and take my land.

Prayer: *Thank you, Lord, that you have set me apart for your purpose, a purpose that flows from my identity in you. When I reflect your nature—your goodness, your kindness, and your love—I proclaim who you are. May others be drawn to the beauty of your character and discover their inheritance in you.*

For Further Reflection:

Psalm 16:5–9
Psalm 105:1–4
Ephesians 2:8–10

Day 43

"Watch and pray so that you will not fall into temptation. The spirit is willing, but the flesh is weak."

Matthew 26:41 (NIV)

In the coming days, it is important to spend time with me in prayer and watch with me. A time of great temptation is coming upon the earth. Those who watch with me and pray will not enter into that temptation. Yes, I can rescue you from temptation and the sin it causes. But it would be better not to enter into temptation at all.

Pray that you do not enter into temptation. Remember the Lord's Prayer. One request is to not enter into temptation but be delivered from evil. Pray this, and I will do it. Pray that you do not enter into temptation.

Prayer: *Thank you, Lord, for teaching me how to watch and pray so I will not enter into temptation. Thank you for faithfully watching over me and guiding me with your unfailing love.*

For Further Reflection:

Matthew 6:6–15
1 Corinthians 10:13
James 1:12–18

Day 44

"They are not of the world, just as I am not of the world."

John 17:16 (NKJV)

Do not be distracted by the things around you or be entangled in the affairs of this world that do not bring you life. Come out from among them. You will walk through the world, use the things of the world, but not be of the world.

No longer will my people be entangled. No longer will my people be ensnared. Instead, my people will be free to worship me alone and serve the people I have made.

No longer will my people be divided between two masters. No longer. For I am a jealous God. I love you, and I desire your love. I will enable you to love and serve me. But I will no longer tolerate a mixture. I will purify my church and make her holy, for I am holy.

You shall be a separated people. You will proclaim the difference between good and evil, right and wrong, the holy and the profane—through your lives, not just your words. You should not have to say a word, but your lives and actions should be enough to convict anyone who is truly seeking me.

Prayer: *Lord, through your unfailing love, you free me from the distractions and snares of the world so I may love and serve you. Thank you for helping me to walk with you in freedom and holiness. May my life be a witness of your goodness and truth so others may be drawn to you.*

For Further Reflection:

Matthew 16:24–27
2 Corinthians 6:16–18
1 John 2:15–17

Day 45

Love is patient and kind. Love is not jealous or boastful or proud or rude. It does not demand its own way. It is not irritable, and it keeps no record of being wronged.

1 Corinthians 13:4–5 (NLT)

Long ago, I said offenses must come. The love of many will grow cold. Offenses will come, but woe to those by whom the offense comes. This is why you should pray for the offender. This is the reason each of my people should attempt to become healers, to stop the cracks when they come to you and allow them to go no further. You can carry it on by gossip, slander, or libel. Or you can cover your brothers and sisters in love. Love covers a multitude of sins and provides healing for the cracks so that my people may be made whole.

I am calling each one of you to say to the cracks, "Stop here! It stops with me." I am calling each one of you to be healers. I am asking you to love those who are injured so that they will not cause injury to someone else. Stop the fractures. Heal the hurt. You can do it. I have placed the ability in you. Refuse to become part of the bitterness, hatred, and unforgiveness that stem from hurt, fear, anger, and unbelief.

Let me heal through you. You can carry this ministry of reconciliation everywhere you go: into your homes, schools, jobs, church, and family. Remember to pray. There is no hurt too old for me to heal, no division too big for me to overcome. I just ask you to love my people. Put your arms around them, hold them, and heal them. Give them something to emulate, imitate, and work toward. Show them who I am, for I am the God who is love.

You think you cannot do this. It's too big a job. I know you cannot do it. All I ask is that you learn to pray and allow me to fill you with my presence and love. Ask me to let my love flow through you when you do not feel loving, when you feel vengeful, hateful, and vindictive. I can still flow through you. Just ask me, and you will find yourself feeling and saying things you would not normally feel or say. Just ask me, so the world can know that I sent my Son and that I love them.

Prayer: *Thank you, Lord, for helping me pause before I react when I feel offended and unloving toward others. Since you have forgiven me, you enable me to forgive those who hurt me. Instead of adding to their pain, may I offer your healing and hope. Thank you for placing your love in me so I can love others.*

For Further Reflection:

Luke 6:27–28
Ephesians 4:29–32
1 Peter 4:8–11

Day 46

Trust in the Lord with all your heart; do not depend on your own understanding. Seek his will in all you do, and he will show you which path to take.

Proverbs 3:5–6 (NLT)

In the coming days, focus your eyes on me. Focus on me. Learn from me. Learn about me. Trust me. I can lead you into the places you need to go in order for you to be all I've called you to be. If you focus on me instead of each other and yourselves, I will lead you to the right place, at the right time, and to the right people. You will then do what I have designed for you from all eternity, the purpose that only you were designed for.

Do not concentrate on others or what I do with others. Concentrate on me. I will bring my purpose to pass. If you find yourself struggling, you will know you have shifted your focus to something other than me. Just shift it back and know I will handle the times and the boundaries. If you focus on me and follow me, you will walk into the places I have designed for you. Your life is not over; it is just beginning. You have not seen all I can do through you, for you, and in you.

Prayer: *Lord, when I am struggling, remind me to turn my focus back to you. I trust you to lead me to the right people and the right places in your perfect timing so that I will accomplish all you have planned.*

For Further Reflection:

Isaiah 26:3–4
Jeremiah 29:11–13
Ephesians 2:10

Day 47

"I am coming to you now, but I say these things while I am still in the world, so that they may have the full measure of my joy within them."

John 17:13 (NIV)

If only my people would understand the joy I placed in them when I came to live in them. A joy that flows out like a river to a world filled with hopelessness and despair. I placed the joy in you when I came to live inside of you. My presence brings the joy. With my joy, you can face trials, warfare, and seeming defeat. But for you, there is no defeat. We win.

If only my people would know and understand. They could share this unlimited supply of joy. As you partake of my joy, it grows and flows to the next person, and the next person, and the next person. Even the ones who do not understand why but only know they feel better. They will feel better because of the joy that is in you. The joy that is in them, as I am in them.

Prayer: *Lord, you enable me to face any trial with joy because you are with me. In your presence is fullness of joy. May your joy flow through me to the hopeless and hurting, to all those who need you and the joy that is found in your presence.*

For Further Reflection:

Psalm 16:11
John 15:9–11
Romans 15:13

Day 48

From the ends of the earth I call to you,
call as my heart grows faint; lead me
to the rock that is higher than I.

Psalm 61:2 (NIV)

My child, keep your eyes on me. When you cannot see me clearly, look to the place you last saw me. Go back there. Seek me. Keep your eyes on me. I will lead you higher, even though it does not seem like that, because my path always leads upward. I am leading you from strength to strength. I am leading you from faith to faith. I am leading you from glory to glory. I am leading you further and further into my image. I am making you more able to do what I can do. But it often seems to you that the path turns downward, and the way gets hard because what was old is useless and dry. New growth is made in my image. New growth is eternal. New growth will not pull you down or weigh you down.

Trust me. Look to me and follow me. The way may not be easy, but others have gone before you, and they made it. So will you. I gave you hind's feet so you will not fall. Even though the way may seem perpendicular, I will keep you on the path. Can you not hear me say to you, "Come up higher," and whisper it into your soul? Each one hears it, but sometimes they think they are imagining it because my voice is not strident but low and not commanding. The drawing power of my voice is without equal. All my people hear my voice. Some of them obey it. My voice is worth obeying. I say to my church, "Come up higher." Live where I live instead of in the valley where the world lives.

Prayer: *Thank you, Lord, that hearing your voice is my heritage as your beloved child. I will listen as you call me to come higher so I can see my circumstances from your perspective. In your presence, I am changed into your image.*

For Further Reflection:

Isaiah 30:18–21
John 10:27–30
2 Corinthians 3:17–18

Day 49

"No eye has seen, no ear has heard, and no mind has imagined what God has prepared for those who love him."

1 Corinthians 2:9 (NLT)

My child, I desire to give you many things, so many things—blessings you cannot imagine, conceive, or understand. But nothing I give you is yours to keep. It is not that I want to take it back, but I want you to pass it on. The flow of blessings in your life should be constant, always filled with good things, constantly changing. I have an unending supply of blessings for you. It is not necessary to hang on to everything I give you because there is more where that came from. The more you pass to others, the more I give to you. I am constantly blessing.

You fear if you let go of the blessings, there will be no more. Let go of the fear. There will be other blessings. My plans are big and vast. You cannot conceive of them or understand all I wish to do for you.

Let go of fear. Let go of the blessings, or they will

own you. The blessings own you if you cling to them. They become your life instead of me. If you hold on to me, there will be blessings—continual, changing—renewed every morning. Just as my mercies are renewed every morning.

You do not have to live on yesterday's manna. Manna turns to worms and becomes dry as dust in your mouth. You do not understand how something you thought would bless you forever could become dry and dusty. Let it go. Pass it on. There is no shortage in my storehouse of blessings for you. Even though you may go through hard times, my plan is to bless you with graces, revelation, and the knowledge you need to get through the hard times.

I never meant for you to stay in a place where a blessing becomes stagnant. Your whole life is a pilgrimage. Let go of the blessings so I can give you more. Let your old blessings be someone else's new. Your life is a river of my supply.

Prayer: Lord, you are so good to me. Thank you for all the blessings you continually give me—wonderful gifts I never dreamed possible. May I be a conduit, sharing your blessings with those you place in my path.

For Further Reflection:

Lamentations 3:22–26
Luke 6:38
James 1:17

Day 50

"When you are brought before synagogues, rulers and authorities, do not worry about how you will defend yourselves or what you will say, for the Holy Spirit will teach you at that time what you should say."

Luke 12:11–12 (NIV)

I tell you the time is coming, and has come for some, when you will be called to stand for what I proclaim as right. You will be called upon to identify yourself with my name. All around you is the pressure to be like everyone else. You may feel fear, doubt, and unbelief. In the end, because of your choice to follow and believe me, out of your mouth will come words that are not your own, but my Spirit's. The doubt and indecision will leave. You will find yourself listening to words coming out of your mouth and say, "Surely, this is not me!" You may experience doubt, fear, and uncertainty. But deep within, you will be at peace. This peace will remain when you speak for me.

The time is come, and will come, for many others to stand up for what they believe. I have made you different, not like everyone else, so you will be a witness to what I have done and what I will do. What you have seen before is a small taste of what is to come.

My power is about to break forth. My presence shall be manifested—seen and felt. You will see the *shekinah* glory of the Lord that overshadowed the Israelites and many others in the past. Even Jesus. This glory will overshadow my people and bring healing, strength, joy, and the ability to stand out when they want to be like others. The ability to be my people instead of their own persons.

There is no reason to fear. The one who taught Moses to speak will give you the words to speak. Do not fear that the darkness is increasing. As the darkness increases, your light shines brighter. The light of the righteous shines brighter than the noonday sun.

Do not fear. When you walk with me, you will never walk in darkness. Let your light be seen so others can walk in that light. The light that you shine will cause others to come to me, know me, and walk in my protection—the protection of the Lord God Almighty. This is my purpose for allowing the darkness to grow—so that my Son can be seen. In the darkness, he shines brighter. Do not put your light under a bushel but on a lampstand for all to see so they will see my Son, who died for them.

Prayer: Lord, you will give me the courage to stand out and stand for you amid adversity. I trust you to give me words to speak that testify of your goodness and mercy. Thank you for your presence and your power, which will shine on your people, bringing healing, strength, and joy.

For Further Reflection:

Isaiah 60:1–3
2 Corinthians 4:6–7
Colossians 3:1–4

Day 51

I can do all this through him
who gives me strength.

Philippians 4:13 (NIV)

Some people in my church are saying, "I can't go on. I can't do this anymore." But I say to you—seek my face. Remember who I am. I am your strength. My strength is in you, and my strength is made perfect in weakness. Your life is in me, and I am in you. Remember that I am for you and not against you. Remember that my grace is sufficient, and my mercies are new every morning. My faithfulness is constant. I am your rearguard, your guide, and your Savior.

I can deliver you out of those things and from the things that cause you to say that you cannot go on. Remember, my Word says, "Many are the afflictions of the righteous, but the LORD delivers you out of them all."[2] Not *some*, but *all*. Remember that I said there would be

---

2 Psalm 34:19 ESV

tribulation in the world, but I have overcome the world, and through me, you have overcome too. There is nothing that you pass through that I will not enable you to endure. I will not allow you to be tried beyond your strength. I am the deliverer in and from temptation.

Remember, look to me and not to yourselves for power and strength. Put your trust in me and not in your resources or in the resources of those around you. Do not put your trust in the things other people trust in. Lean fully on me. I am able to bring you victory in every situation and every trial.

Prayer: Lord, you have gone before me in every circumstance I face, and your presence goes with me. Thank you for giving me strength to overcome every obstacle and every temptation. I trust that you are able to bring me victory in every trial. You are faithful.

For Further Reflection:

Psalm 34:17–19
Romans 8:31–39
2 Corinthians 12:9–10

Day 52

Let us run with endurance the race that is set before us, looking unto Jesus, the author and finisher of our faith.

Hebrews 12:1–2 (NKJV)

Lift your eyes. Look to me. Do not turn away from me. Keep yourself focused. How do you keep your focus from wavering? Keep your eyes on me. Do not look at your circumstances. Do not take notice of what the Enemy is doing. Look at me and what I am doing. Let your lips speak of what I am doing.

I will hold you still and keep you whole and united. The wisdom you need will come. You will know what to do, how to do it, and you will be excited about doing it with me. You will walk a new path. You will be excited and not afraid. You will anticipate what is ahead. Even if there are obstacles, I will enable you to overcome them. I will not let you start out and leave you unable to reach your destination. Whether there are storms ahead or you're walking on water, I'm in the midst. Look at these times as an adventure.

Prayer: Thank you for helping me focus on your goodness and beauty instead of my circumstances. You give me the wisdom I need to overcome any obstacle I face. Instead of fear, I will look upon our adventure with excitement as you teach me how to be an overcomer.

For Further Reflection:

1 Chronicles 16:8–12
Proverbs 3:5–6
Colossians 1:9–12

Day 53

But he said to me, "My grace is sufficient for you, for my power is made perfect in weakness." Therefore I will boast all the more gladly about my weaknesses, so that Christ's power may rest on me.

2 Corinthians 12:9 (NIV)

Do not be afraid. Do not be afraid, for no matter what comes against you, my grace is sufficient. Where sin abounds, my grace abounds more. I have great plans for each one of you, and my grace is sufficient to get you there.

Do not be afraid. Look to me and trust me to take you to the places you cannot go alone. I need each of you to do what I ask. I am able to take you to the places you need to go and equip you with what you need.

There is no need to fear. Repent—align your thoughts with mine—and I will change you. I will take you where you need to go. Trust me. Rejoice even in your failures and weaknesses, for it is in these things that I am seen the most.

Prayer: *Lord, I trust you to equip me and take me to the places you want me to go. As I align my thoughts with yours, I will think as you think. I will be able see from your perspective and rejoice, even when I see no reason to rejoice. I have no cause to fear, for you are always with me.*

For Further Reflection:

Deuteronomy 31:8
Acts 3:19–21
Romans 5:20–21

Day 54

"Just as Moses lifted up the snake in the wilderness, so the Son of Man must be lifted up, that everyone who believes may have eternal life in him."

John 3:14–15 (NIV)

Long ago in a desert, I told my people to lift up a serpent on a brass pole, and if they looked at it, they would live. It was a symbol of the cross. If you look upon the cross with faith, there is life for you. Salvation, healing, and saving power from the fires of hell. There is deliverance and freedom in the cross.

Do not fear the cross, but join yourself to it. You will find the freedom you seek and have not found anywhere else. If you look and want to be healed from the bite of the serpent, the bite of the devil, look at the cross with faith. Look at it, and you shall live.

Look closely at the cross. You will see that it is not smooth or pretty. It is rough, splintered, bloody, and cruel. What the nails did not do, the cross finished. It finished tearing the skin off my Son's back as he pushed himself up and down. Part of his skin came off his back, his arms, his legs, and his body. It was not pretty. An instrument of death but adorned with a priceless jewel.

The cross was adorned with my Son, adorned with his body, adorned with the divine Savior, adorned with the one who died so you might live. He died so you might be healed, so that you might be free. Indeed, even at his bloodiest, he was beautiful, precious, lovely, and beyond description.

This is my beloved. This is your friend, and his desire is toward you.

Prayer: Lord, I cannot fathom the depth of your suffering. I am grateful you loved me so much that you died for me so we could live together as one. You paid the price to set me free from sin, guilt, and shame, and instead, you enable me to live a new life in oneness with you.

For Further Reflection:

Isaiah 52:13–53:12
Romans 8:1–4
1 Peter 2:21–25

Day 55

"And He has made from one blood every nation of men to dwell on all the face of the earth, and has determined their preappointed times and the boundaries of their dwellings, so that they should seek the Lord, in the hope that they might grope for Him and find Him, though He is not far from each one of us; for in Him we live and move and have our being."

Acts 17:26–28 (NKJV)

I, the Lord, have determined boundaries, times, and works for you to do. I have done this not because I needed you to do works but so my kingdom would be established on earth as it is in heaven. I have done this so each of you would need to seek me.

If you wonder why you are placed where you are, I placed you there so that you will seek me. I said this in Acts 17. More than anything, I desire that you seek me so that you will live with me. Even if you seek me in the most elementary way, or in any way at all, I will be found, as long as your heart is in the seeking. I am not so far away, as you might think, but as close as the next breath you draw. And more than that, I want to be found by you.

It is to your benefit that I cause you to seek me. I put a place in you that only I can satisfy. I made you in such a way that you value what you work for. You do not value what is easy to get. All who seek will find. I promised this from the mouth of my own Son.

Your circumstances are not random. Your life is not an accident. My hand is on your life and all your circumstances. I work to my own purpose even what the Enemy has done so that you will seek me. In everyone's life, there are things the Enemy has done, but this does not deflect my purpose. I knew what he would do in advance. But I protect you, for I have placed boundaries on him too. My Son prayed that you would be kept from the Evil One, so I designed the boundaries for your protection. Your life is precious. I could leave nothing to chance.

You made choices that affect your life. Some things I left to your choice, but nothing is done by chance. All is done in love because I want you to know me. And I want to know you.

Prayer: *Lord, as I seek you, you reveal yourself to me. I am honored that you desire to live with and in me. Thank you for leaving nothing concerning me to chance. I am so precious to you that you designed boundaries to protect me.*

For Further Reflection:

Isaiah 55:6–9
Jeremiah 29:11–13
John 17:3

Day 56

"Even now my witness is in heaven; my advocate is on high. My intercessor is my friend as my eyes pour out tears to God; on behalf of a man he pleads with God as one pleads for his friend."

Job 16:19–21 (NIV)

I have raised up intercessors. I have made them champions for those who cannot fight for themselves. I have strengthened them and taught them to fight, to go forth, and to stand in the gap to rescue those who cannot rescue themselves. There is no longer any area of the world that does not have intercessors. I am raising up strengthened intercessors to go forth.

They shall rise up and face the Enemy without fear. Even his power is not great enough to deter the people in my church. In every corner, crevice, and every part of the world, all will know that I am the Lord your God, and there is nothing that I cannot do. No one will be forgotten or disenfranchised, for I am the Lord your God, your hope, your restoration, and your wholeness.

I come on a mighty wave of prayer. My intercessors carry me wherever they go.

My intercessors will see great things. The Enemy shall be stripped of his power. And power shall be restored to those who are made in my image. They will become all I meant them to be because my intercessors will not be afraid to voice what they see. I will put the words in their mouths. They will pray my Word and proclaim it in every corner of the world, and my hope will come to the earth. No one will be left out.

I will be lifted high, and they shall say, "There is a God." I will restore and create life where there was no life. People will know that I am God and there is no other. I will be lifted up.

Prayer: Lord, you live to intercede for us, and you have given me the privilege of praying with you. You strengthen me, guide me, and give me your heart and your words to pray on behalf of those who cannot fight for themselves. No one is forgotten, abandoned, or left behind. Thank you for those intercessors whom you have called to pray for me when I need prayer.

For Further Reflection:

Romans 8:26–27
Ephesians 6:18
Hebrews 7:23–25

Day 57

"So do not fear, for I am with you; do not be dismayed, for I am your God. I will strengthen you and help you; I will uphold you with my righteous right hand."

Isaiah 41:10 (NIV)

Do not be afraid. Do not be afraid. I am with you. Yes, I care for you. I know the boat is rocking. I know about your storm on the sea, but I have made provision for you. I have given you the command to cross to the other side. You will cross. You will get to the other side.

I am in the boat with you. I may not be visible to you, just as I seemed invisible to the disciples in the boat while I was sleeping. I am telling you what I told them—believe. Have faith. You will not capsize in the storm. I am in control of this boat. I am in control of your lives, and you will not capsize in the storm. I want you to know how much I love you, care for you, and how much I want to take care of you.

Prayer: *Thank you, Lord, that you understand how I feel. You experienced every aspect of our humanity, yet you never yielded to fear or doubt. You believed the Word of the Father and rested in his love and provision for you. Just as the Father was with you, so you will be with me and provide for me through every storm and every challenge.*

For Further Reflection:

Psalm 57:1–3
Isaiah 43:1–2
Mark 4:35–41

Day 58

God has said, "Never will I leave you; never will I forsake you."

Hebrews 13:5 (NIV)

Listen, my people, to what I am saying. My army is not like other armies. In my army, I lead. I leave no one behind, leave no one wounded, nor do I leave bodies for the Enemy to collect. If my people do not find every wounded person, I do. My angels do. My Spirit goes back and forth over the earth looking for those who fear the Lord. No matter how wounded, how scarred, how they look to the world, or how unprofitable they may look or seem, I leave no one behind.

The ones my people do not find, I go back and pick up. Remember this in the days to come. I never leave the wounded or dead. For precious in the eyes of the Lord is the death of his saints. I leave nothing for the Enemy.

In the days to come, if you feel wounded and no one comes looking, I will come. I know where you are. But I give my people a chance to come looking so they will be blessed by ministering to you and receive a reward.

Do not be afraid of being left behind or think that your life means nothing to me. Even your death is precious to me, and you shall not be left in the Enemy's hands. You will be picked up and taken to my throne by my angels. Even if my people fail you, I will never fail you.

This will be important in the days to come because war will be all around, and the Enemy will make you feel afraid and outgunned. He will tell you that you are forgotten. But you are not forgotten. I know where you are. Your position has not been forgotten. The Enemy does not have all the ammunition he lets you think he has. He makes a lot of noise, but do not be distracted by the Enemy's volume. The little you think you have, if applied, can overcome him.

I will not leave you an orphan or abandon you, for I will come myself. But I warn you, the warfare each of you experiences will increase. It will seem as if there are more against you than for you. You must remember, I leave no wounded, no bodies. I am the resurrection and the life, and everywhere I go, there is life brought forth.

You are not forgotten, overlooked, or ill-equipped. I have equipped all my soldiers with the same equipment. Learn to use it. The Enemy's strongest weapons cannot overcome the seemingly little you think you have. I will back you.

Prayer: *Lord, you promise never to leave me or forsake me. Help me to remember that no matter what happens, I am not forgotten or left behind. You always come for me. May I reach out with your love to others who may feel lost and alone.*

For Further Reflection:

Psalm 91:1–16
Isaiah 49:14–16
Ephesians 6:10–18

Day 59

The LORD is my light and my salvation—
whom shall I fear? The LORD is the stronghold
of my life—of whom shall I be afraid?

Psalm 27:1 (NIV)

Remember, my child, do not fear evil. Remember to overcome evil with good. Do not fear evil, for I am with you. I am with every single one of you. Even if you are walking in the shadow of death, you are walking with me. I am the resurrection.

Do not be afraid of the darkness around you, for even the smallest light becomes powerful in darkness. Do not be afraid of the darkness. I am the light, and you are light. The light shines brighter the darker it gets around you. The darkness will be driven back by the light in you, the light of my own Son, the light that is in me. In the end, the area around you will seem bright as noonday, without even a shadow. The dark and the light are both alike to me.

You have nothing to fear, for I am here. There is nowhere you can go where I do not go as well. There is no darkness or evil stronger than my power within you. The key is to remember it is *my power*. It is not dependent on you.

I warn you: the darkness is coming. The warfare will seem stronger. But I tell you, you have nothing to fear. I will not abandon you. The Enemy lies about his resources and power. Do not believe all you hear. Remember to look to me. I will keep you in perfect peace.

Prayer: Lord, I will not fear darkness or evil because you are with me. You are the light that overcomes all darkness. Thank you for your peace that calms my heart even during tumultuous times.

For Further Reflection:

Joshua 1:9
Isaiah 26:3–4
John 8:12

Day 60

You are my hiding place; you will protect me from trouble and surround me with songs of deliverance.

Psalm 32:7 (NIV)

Don't you realize, my child, I never surround you to limit you? I never surround you to make it hard for you. I surround you to protect you. I surround you so you will get to know my presence—so you will realize who I am and come to know me. For you are drawn to my presence just as the deer is drawn to water. Your soul longs for me.

You do not have fences or boundaries created by human hands, but supernatural boundaries made by my hands. Can't you rejoice in this instead of rebelling against it? Rejoice in it, for I am the one who determines your places and times. I walk with you. I go with you behind and before to hedge you in, not with circumstances, rules, and regulations, but with myself and with my angels.

If there are rules, they are to give you visible signs of my presence. For you see, wherever I am is holy. My presence makes everything holy. My rules—the few I do require—are only to keep all things holy. I want to protect you from the consequences of evil just as a parent does. I am the one who protects you and surrounds you.

Prayer: Lord, you continually draw me to yourself with your lovingkindness. I am grateful you love me so much that you surround me with your protection and your presence. May my trust in you grow as I rejoice in your perfect wisdom.

For Further Reflection:

Psalm 63:1–5
John 15:9–11
Acts 17:26–28

Day 61

You are altogether beautiful, my darling; there is no flaw in you.

Song of Songs 4:7 (NIV)

My children, listen to me. Turn your eyes upon me and look upon my glory, my beauty, my majesty, and my greatness. Whenever you turn your eyes to yourself, you will find yourself lacking. There is never a time you are blemished if you look at me and exalt in the beauty you see when you look at me. You will hear me say, "No spot or blemish is in you." I am completely captivated by your love for me. I say there is no wrong in you.

You may not understand my Word. Though at times it may seem contradictory, the whole of my Word is truth. If you look at me, you will understand that the one who loves you just as you are makes you worthy. I love you, redeemed you, and washed you in the blood of my Son. There is no one unworthy. Look at me. Look at who I am. I tell you who you are. You tell others who I am, and I will tell them who they are.

Prayer: *Thank you, Lord, that when you look at me, you find no fault in me. You always see me through your eyes of love—beautiful, redeemed, and cleansed by your blood.*

For Further Reflection:

Psalm 145:1–5
2 Corinthians 3:17–18
Colossians 1:13–14

Day 62

"Blessed are those who listen to me, watching daily at my doors, waiting at my doorway. For those who find me find life and receive favor from the LORD."

Proverbs 8:34–35 (NIV)

My people, keep your eyes on me. When you first turn your eyes toward me, they don't seem to focus because I am so different. But as you look at me, I give you the ability to focus. What do you see? A God dried up and old? No, you see the same God who makes all things new. The God who died on the cross, resurrected from the dead, and who remains as powerful today as he was when he walked on the earth and is now seated on his throne. This is the God who created you, thought about you, and planned for you. I am always new, creating, healing, and restoring.

Look away from the things of the world and everyday life. In the parable of the sower, I warned you that everyday life would choke the seed of the Word. Do not look at the circumstances of your life. Look at me. Let me walk with you through your daily life. Let me do life with you, through you, and for you. From the simplest to the hardest, I delight in doing wonderful things for my people.

I search the earth for a people who look to me so I can show myself to them. I have miracles you could never dream of. Look for me. Watch for me. Do not do life alone. Make me a part of your life. Rejoice in me, not in your circumstances or blessings. Rejoice in me and be thankful that I have given you eternal life and have written your names down in heaven.

My plans are bigger than you could ever think or dream. Keep your eyes on me. Praise me. Trust me. I will never leave you to walk through this life alone in your own strength, without help.

Prayer: Lord, you are a powerful and majestic God. Yet you are the same God who lives in me and delights in healing me and restoring me. You lovingly make plans for my life and shower me with your blessings. Though I rejoice in all you have done for me, I rejoice even more in who you are.

For Further Reflection:

Luke 8:4–15
Ephesians 3:14–21
1 Peter 1:3–9

Day 63

For our struggle is not against flesh and blood, but against the rulers, against the authorities, against the powers of this dark world and against the spiritual forces of evil in the heavenly realms.

Ephesians 6:12 (NIV)

I am present with you. I have come as a victorious, conquering king to strengthen each one in my church. A battle rages and is still going on. I need each of my warriors in top condition: knowing who I am, ready to follow where I lead without fear, and knowing I have won the victory.

The Enemy is cruel, cunning, and strong. But you are stronger, for you have my power. My Spirit will give you courage, power, and strength, which come from me—from my throne. Nothing shall stand before me. You will win the battle. You will win the war. It is done. It is finished. Now go and enforce the victory.

Just as the Egyptian horses and their riders were thrown into the sea, so your enemies will be thrown into the sea of fire. They will not prevail. My church will stand. My people will show them that what I have done is final. My people will proclaim my victory, display it, and rejoice in it.

The Enemy knows that his defeat is final. Do not be afraid of his anger or craft, for I am stronger than he and wiser than he. He is a created being. He is not my equal. He would like you to think he is my equal, or close to it. But he is far from my equal.

I could do this myself, but I want you to know and experience the glory of defeating the one who has tried to defeat you. I want you to have the elation of knowing that my grace and judgment can flow through you. Judgment against the Enemy, not against the people I have created, known, and loved. I will heal them if they let me. I will restore them if they accept me. There is no redemption or restoration for the Enemy. Nothing but failure, loss, and eternal doom. He has nothing. I am the one whom you shall fear. Not in the way you fear him but because of who I am.

Do not waste your strength and time fighting with each other. Pour all your strength into this battle against the Enemy, not against brothers and sisters or unbelievers. Fight without fear, knowing the victory is guaranteed. No weapon formed against you will prosper.

Prayer: Lord, help me to remember that the battles I fight are not against people, but against the Enemy. Thank you for defeating the Enemy on the cross and granting me the privilege of sharing in that victory with you.

For Further Reflection:

Luke 10:17–20
Romans 8:37–39
Colossians 2:11–15

Day 64

But the one who rules in heaven laughs.

Psalm 2:4 (NLT)

I know you may think singing children's songs is silly. But they become alive as you begin to sing the words of the songs. Doors of your heart burst open, and my presence comes in. Joy bursts forth from your lives, a river to an arid and desolate world.

When the Enemy rages, sometimes your best defense is laughter. He hates that. I laugh at him, and you can laugh at him too. The Enemy hates my laughter, and he will hate yours.

Don't despise the children's songs. They are often the very thing to open your hearts to great joy and strength in the battle.

Prayer: *Thank you, Lord, for giving us laughter and songs to use as weapons against the Enemy. When the Enemy rages, may my mouth be filled with laughter and my lips with songs of joy.*

For Further Reflection:

Job 8:20–21
Psalm 126:1–3
Colossians 3:16

Day 65

"My sheep listen to my voice; I know them, and they follow me. I give them eternal life, and they shall never perish; no one can snatch them out of my hand."

John 10:27–28 (NIV)

I am indeed holy, far above what you understand or know. Yet I am as near to you as your next breath. The God who created the universe lives inside of you. I am the God who sent my Son to die for the whole world. I care about everything that happens to you, every minute of every day. I am interested in my people—what they want, and what they say. I want you, my people, to be interested in me as I am in you—in what I want, and what I say.

I am drawing my people to myself. Will you come? I know you can hear me. I know you can feel the drawing power of my Spirit. At various times of the day, you feel me tugging at you to come. I want you to be interested in me, as I am in you. I want you to take part in my plan. I want you to know my plans before they come to pass.

Exalt and worship me. Be filled with my Spirit. I will keep the promises I made to you. Walk close to me and obey my Spirit, and trust that I will keep my Word. What I have done so far is nothing compared to what I will do.

I want you to know me as much as I know you. It is necessary because a time of revival is coming. But there will be great darkness and danger. You must know the difference because the Enemy's power will be great. Some things will look like me, but they will not be me. Get to know my voice while there is still time. Get to know my ways so you can be safe and so that when someone presents a counterfeit, you will know intuitively it is not me. They may act and sound like me, but they do not feel like me—because you know me.

Remember, in the last days, I said there would arise deceiving spirits that would even deceive the elect. Make your election sure by the power of the Holy Spirit. Let him lead you into all truth so that you will know the difference between the truth and a lie.

Prayer: *Lord, you are a holy God, worthy of all honor and praise. Yet you care for me and draw me deeper into your presence through your lovingkindness. Thank you for giving me your Holy Spirit to lead me into your truth and guard me from deception. I trust you to fulfill your promises to me. You are faithful.*

For Further Reflection:

Psalm 145:17–19
John 16:12–15
2 Timothy 3:13–17

Day 66

God's purpose in all this was to use the church to display his wisdom in its rich variety to all the unseen rulers and authorities in the heavenly places.

Ephesians 3:10 (NLT)

I have created each one in my church to magnify my name and show my purpose to the angels, both the good angels and the fallen. They learn about me because of what I have done for you. You are teaching the angels.

My Word says you demonstrate what I am like. The angels watch but do not understand. When the fallen angels see you, they know how much they lost. You see, they have contempt for you. But you can show them who I am and who you are. As you magnify me, lift me up, and acknowledge who I am, you are teaching even my angels—my creation—who I am and who you are.

Prayer: *Lord, I am honored that you have created me in your image and called me to reflect who you are, not only on earth but before the hosts of heaven. I exalt your name, for you deserve all my praise.*

For Further Reflection:

Psalm 8:1–6
Colossians 1:15–18
Hebrews 1:1–14

Day 67

Then Jesus told his disciples a parable to show them that they should always pray and not give up.

Luke 18:1 (NIV)

Children, do not give up. Keep praying. I know my people have prayed prayers they think will never come to pass. Many have abandoned prayers they assumed would not be answered because they have not seen the answer. Keep praying. I must find faith on this earth. A time is coming when the answers to prayers are going to come like drops of rain in a cloudburst. Those prayers that you forgot you prayed or thought would not be answered? They will be answered. Keep praying.

Renew your minds. Renew your minds with my Word. I am not a God who won't save. I am not a God who moves once in a while. Read the Word, and you will see that I am a God who takes part in your daily activities, a God who answers prayers even after you quit praying.

I keep you from evil and redeem you every day. I give you bread every day. Every day, I heal you and crown you with lovingkindness and mercy. I give you good things. I renew your youth like the eagle's every day, if you let me. Every day, open yourselves up to me. I am an *every* day God, not a *sometimes* God.

Prayer: *Thank you, Lord, that you hear every prayer, every cry of my heart. Even while I wait for answers, you fill each day with your blessings, kindness, and mercy. May my heart be full of thanksgiving even before I see the answers to my prayers.*

For Further Reflection:

Psalm 103:1–5
2 Timothy 3:14–17
1 John 5:14–15

Day 68

"I tell you, there is rejoicing in the presence of the angels of God over one sinner who repents."

Luke 15:10 (NIV)

I want you to understand how I rejoice over each person who knows me. I rejoice over every human being who accepts what I have done and who I am. Each one brings me eternal joy. This is the reason I could endure the cross. I saw the joy long before I felt joy. I saw every soul before me. I rejoiced over each one then, and I rejoice over each of you now. They are mine, and you are mine. My Father has given all of you to me. Every time you pray and praise me, I rejoice.

If you understood the source of my joy, you would not think badly of yourself. You bring laughter and joy to our hearts and cause the halls of heaven to ring with laughter. All the saints and angels are rejoicing over each soul who accepts me as their Lord and Savior. I delight over each one.

Each one of you is holy ground, for I am present with you. Each one of you is my temple. Each one of you is my house, and I am your house. You are mine, and I am yours. I make you holy. My presence sanctifies you, for I alone am holy. You cannot make yourself holy. The most you can do is yield yourself to holiness, the fruit it brings forth, and the resulting actions, for I am the one who makes you holy. You are holy.

If you know you need to be cleansed, come to me. I will wash you with my blood and the water of my Word. I restore you to full fellowship with me. I wash away all your sin. I give you my righteousness and clothe you with my sinless nature. You are holy. I make you holy.

Prayer: Jesus, I am amazed that you—the holy God—not only endured the cross so I would be made clean and holy, but you did so with joy, looking forward to my being one with you. I join the chorus of heaven rejoicing over each person who accepts you as their Savior.

For Further Reflection:

Zephaniah 3:17
John 17:13–19
Hebrews 12:1–2

Day 69

And my God will meet all your needs according to the riches of his glory in Christ Jesus.

Philippians 4:19 (NIV)

Do not place me in the past. Many in my church believe I can do anything, but when it comes to their problems, they put me in the past. I did it for your grandmother, mother, or spiritual mother. But do you believe I can do it for you? I am not just God of the past, but I am God of the present. I am the God of your present.

The God who provided in the past will provide now. The God who healed in the past will heal now. The God who led you in the past will lead you now. I have been leading, providing, and healing you. It may not have been the way you thought it would be, but it has brought you to the right place and to the right people.

In the name of my Son, I led you like a shepherd through each wilderness. It may not have been what you wanted, but it was what you needed to be strong in me, for me to lead you into the promised land to fight the giants.

You don't need to fear giants. The battle is proof that I am real and have not changed. I am God of the valleys, God of the mountains, God of the deserts, and God of all the spacious places you love. Love me.

I am God of your present. I can do more than you can think, dream, or imagine. I'm looking for someone to believe in me, to show myself strong on their behalf. I am the God who parted the Red Sea, and I will part it for you if you believe in me. Do not put me in the past, not even your past.

Prayer: *Thank you, Lord, for how you guided me and provided for me in the past. But you are not just the God of my past; you are the God who provides for me in my present. I trust you to lead me into my future—a future filled with healing, provision, restoration, and hope.*

For Further Reflection:

Psalm 23:1–6
Isaiah 30:18–21
Ephesians 3:14–21

Day 70

Little children, let no one deceive you. He who practices righteousness is righteous, just as He is righteous.

1 John 3:7 (NKJV)

Be careful, my church. In the coming days, do not be deceived by those around you who say and do nice things, but in your spirit, something tells you the source is not right. Be careful so as not to be deceived. A spirit of deception is loose in your land. Pay attention to my Spirit deep within you, for my Spirit will guide you through the land mines in the fields around you.

The spirit of deception is growing. Be careful to listen to my Spirit. Seize the time and stand for me. Do not be silent, my church. Tell the people I am God. I love every one of them. I died for them, and I love them. Tell them I am God. There is no other God. There is only me.

***Prayer**: Lord, you have given me your Holy Spirit to guide me into your truth. When something doesn't feel right in my spirit, I ask you for wisdom and discernment. Thank you for helping me live out your truth so others may know you and escape the snares of deception.*

For Further Reflection:

John 16:13–15
Colossians 2:6–10
1 John 4:1–6

Day 71

"And I, when I am lifted up from the earth, will draw all people to myself."

John 12:32 (NIV)

I have determined to lift up and exalt on high the name of my Son. It is the name of my Son I have lifted high, and no one else. It is the name of my Son I have lifted high in this nation. I have designed your nation to lift the name of my Son on high so all may acknowledge him throughout the world. I have blessed this country with wealth to fund my kingdom and minister to those who need my Son everywhere, to reach out and be my hands and heart.

Now, my Son's name is mentioned less and less in this nation and lifted high less and less. This is not what I want. Pray that the name of my Son may once again be lifted up. I want you to be all I made you to be. I want your country to be all I made it to be. I want you to be my hands, heart, and soul to show others who I am. Lift up my name and exalt it high so others may come to know me. Do not hide my name. Do not despise or dishonor my name.

Prayer: *Lord, I lift high your name over my life and my nation. Teach me how to pray for my country so that we may fulfill your divine purpose. Show me how to be an extension of your hands and heart to those around me so that others may exalt your name.*

For Further Reflection:

2 Chronicles 7:14
Psalm 2:6–8
Romans 10:14–17

Day 72

Rescue the weak and the needy; deliver them from the hand of the wicked.

Psalm 82:4 (NIV)

I have assigned each of you a place to defend. Each Christian has an assigned land to defend, and those of you who are intercessors have larger places to defend. You are overseers for those who are weaker or those who are unable to defend themselves. Each of my intercessors has a larger sphere, but each person has a territory to proclaim as mine, for the earth and its fullness is mine.

Your job is to proclaim what is true. Proclaim my will to be done in the area I have given you. I have given each of you a place to stake a claim for my Spirit to go forth throughout the earth and bring people to be healed and discipled. I call each of you to strengthen, heal, and encourage them. I assigned you a territory. I do not mean for you just to stay there, stake it, and claim it as mine, but to go into the Enemy's territory and take back what is mine. Take it back. Bring the people into your sphere to strengthen them and build them up.

Intercessors are responsible for other lives, not just their own. You are the defending army, the foot soldiers who go in and defend. Proclaim that I am Lord wherever you go and enforce my victory wherever you are.

Prayer: Lord, you have given us prayer as a weapon to rescue those oppressed by the Enemy. Show us how to defend those who cannot defend themselves and offer them your comfort and encouragement. Thank you for your Holy Spirit, who helps us pray, not with human understanding but according to your wisdom and divine purpose.

For Further Reflection:

Romans 8:26–27
Ephesians 6:18
2 Corinthians 2:14

Day 73

"I saw the Lord always before me. Because he is at my right hand, I will not be shaken."

Acts 2:25 (NIV)

I am deep inside you. Rest in me. Do not let the everyday circumstances of life rob you, worry you, or trouble you. Reach deep within to where I am. You will find an abiding peace that cannot be taken from you, a joy that cannot be robbed, and a strength that remains available to you always. When you find yourself on shaky ground, take a deep breath and look for me. I am still there. I have not changed. I have promised you the kingdom.

Many of the things you see around you are not of my kingdom. They can be shaken, destroyed, and torn down. I promised you in the past that everything that can be shaken will be shaken. In the end, everything that remains is part of my kingdom. When you find yourself on shaky ground, you are looking at your circumstances and have allowed the Enemy to confuse you.

When the shaking comes, look to me. I will be there. Do not lean on your own understanding. Acknowledge me. I will make your paths straight. I will make straight not just some ways, but all ways: the easy ways, the hard ways, the ways you understand, and the ones you don't. I will direct your paths. You will not be moved or shaken. Everything around you might be shaken, but you will not be shaken.

Prayer: Lord, help me to remember that when my world is shaken by worries or troubles, you have promised me your peace. Instead of allowing stress to overwhelm me, I will rest safe and secure in you, knowing your love for me never changes. You will lead me and guide me through these troubles and strengthen me with your joy.

For Further Reflection:

Proverbs 3:5–6
John 16:33
Hebrews 12:26–28

Day 74

Now thanks be to God who always leads us in triumph in Christ.

2 Corinthians 2:14 (NKJV)

Church, listen to me. Rise up and stand. Rise up and fight. Rise up and triumph. Do not look to the left or to the right to determine what your circumstances are or how things seem to be going. Do not say, "I cannot stand." I will enable you to stand, fight, win, and walk in triumph—a triumph unlike any you have seen or experienced in your life.

You look to your circumstances to see if I have done this or that. But do not look to your circumstances. Rise up, my church, rise up. Do not let the Enemy destroy you and determine what will happen, for my purpose will be accomplished on earth as it is in heaven. Walk in confidence and faith. Look at me. Do not look at those around you, your circumstances, or your feelings.

You will walk in places you have never walked before. You will not walk in fear. You will walk in confidence because I will protect you. Keep your eyes on me. My church will not be defeated. No weapon formed against you will prosper. You must learn to trust, believe, and look to my Word and depend on what it says. You will not be surrounded by depression, fear, or anxiety as you walk through life. But you will be surrounded and protected by my blood, my name, and my Word. The angels hasten to do my bidding to support you and make sure my Word comes to pass.

Do not depend on what you see and hear, but depend on me and my provision. My church must learn to stand, trust, and believe in me. You will rejoice and encourage yourself in me even when the same circumstances cause others to be tearful and afraid.

Prayer: Thank you, Lord, that you empower me to stand on the truth of your Word when difficulties arise. You have provided perfect protection for me by your Word, your name, and your blood. You even send your angels to help me. Therefore, I refuse to entertain negative thoughts from the Enemy—fear, depression, or anxiety—that seek to defeat me. I trust you to lead me to triumph over every adversity.

For Further Reflection:

Psalm 112:4–8
Isaiah 54:17
1 Corinthians 16:13–14

Day 75

"Do not tremble; do not be afraid. Did I not proclaim my purposes for you long ago? You are my witnesses."

Isaiah 44:8 (NLT)

If each of you desires to be lifted out of the place where you are, where is the witness to those around you? If I take you out of every situation that seems hard, how will you be my witness? Doesn't my Word say you are a witness? How will those people know me? The things that terrify everyone else will not terrify you. I have sent you to the places where you live and work to proclaim the news that I have come to be with them.

You are light, as I am the light. All those without the light gather around you, and they question deep within their hearts, "Why are they different from me and from all of us? Why do they remain peaceful and strong in this situation that makes us fear and quake? Why are they different? Why does the darkness that covers us not affect them?"

Remember the prayer of Saint Francis: "Lord, make me an instrument of your peace: where there is hatred, let me sow love."[3] Wherever you are, you are put there to be the source of the very thing opposite of that which opposes you. You are a source of blessing, change, and peace within the situation. I am the source of life, peace, and blessing within you. Let my presence, my strength, and my peace flow freely in the situations I put you in. Let me cleanse, change, and uplift that situation. Do not become part of the world around you. Let me use you to redeem the time you live in.

Prayer: Lord, you empower me to react to my circumstances in ways that are different from the world. Since you live in me, you teach me to respond from my new nature: peace, love, joy, and kindness. You have called me to be your light, bringing your peace into places of chaos. Thank you, Lord, that through your presence in me, I am a source of blessing to those around me.

For Further Reflection:

Isaiah 43:10–12
John 17:13–19
Ephesians 5:8–10

3 "Prayers," compiled by Rev. Hiram Brett, Chaplain, Connecticut Mental Health Center, PDF document, Yale School of Medicine, accessed September 10, 2025, https://files-profile.medicine.yale.edu/documents/c461a68f-fd78-4362-a247-8c7baf7fb31d/.

Day 76

*"Write the vision And make it plain on tablets,
That he may run who reads it. For the vision is yet
for an appointed time; But at the end it will speak,
and it will not lie. Though it tarries, wait for it;
Because it will surely come, It will not tarry."*

Habakkuk 2:2–3 (NKJV)

Go back to the vision I gave you. Do not let it go. Wait for it. It will not be late. Do not let go of the promises I have given you, for the promises are greater than you understand. They reach far into the world and into my kingdom. They are a bridge between the world and my kingdom. The vision I have given you is part of my plan. Go back, review it, and ask me to help you understand. Plan for it; prepare for it, for it will come to pass. It will not be late.

Be careful. Do not steady yourself on anything around you. Anything around you that is not of me will become shifting sand sooner or later and will not bear your weight. Keep your eyes on me. There is nothing to fear, for I have firmly rooted your feet in grace. I will cause you to stand. I am your strength. When you have no strength, you can call on mine.

Do not fear. Go back to your vision, to the first love you had with me. Let yourself be held in safety within my presence, safe from the trouble all around you. The trouble will not break your peace, for you are safe in my presence. The purpose I have for your life will come to pass if you go back to the original vision I gave you. Spend your time preparing for it by rejoicing in me. Encourage yourself in me. Draw on the Spirit of hope deep within you. I have placed hope in your heart, and that hope will not disappoint you. It will cause you to wait expectantly for me to work in your life.

Prayer: Lord, thank you for the promises you have given me to stand on—promises that reflect your heart, your love, and your hope for my future. Show me how to encourage myself in you, to prepare my heart to receive these wonderful promises. I rejoice in you as I wait in hope. You are faithful.

For Further Reflection:

Psalm 63:7–8
Romans 4:20–21
Hebrews 6:15–19

Day 77

But my eyes are fixed on you, Sovereign
Lord; in you I take refuge.

Psalm 141:8 (NIV)

My child, don't look to your own strength. Don't look to yourself or your own resources. Look to me. Do not proclaim your own weakness unless you claim my strength. Do not proclaim your despair unless it is to state the hope that is in you. When others are terrified, you will walk in safety and peace. Those around you will wonder why, and so will you. Except you know me.

You are not on your own, but I hold each of you in the palm of my hand. You have always been in my hand, but from this time on, you will know it.

Rule upon rule and precept upon precept, I will teach you. I love you and have a plan for you, just as a parent plans for a child. A parent makes provision, and the child walks in the middle of that provision. So will you walk in my provision.

In the coming days, you will learn how complete my protection is for you and how true my promises are. The Word that was always true will come to pass in your life, and the words to your prayers shall go beyond strength and asking. I am your hope, your peace, and your protection. You will have unspeakable joy in the midst of despair, and peace without understanding why. Amid changes, you will walk in peace without turmoil or fear.

Do not look around you, as Peter did in the storm, but keep your eyes on me. As long as you look at me, you will not sink into the fear around you. Keep your eyes on me. I will provide for you, save you, and deliver you. I will do all I promised you. Few of you understand what that promise is, but I will do it anyway. I will open your understanding. I am your hope and your anchor. You will say, as Joshua did at the end of his life, that of all the words the Lord spoke to him, not one failed to be fulfilled.

Be sure to keep your eyes focused on me, not just on the promise, not on people, nor on your circumstances. But keep your eyes focused on me. Ask me to help you. I will reach out my hand to you, and you will walk on the water of your life until we get into the boat together and go over to the other side.

Prayer: *Thank you, Lord, that you are a good Father. With tender love and compassion, you care for me and provide for me. I don't need to fear or fret when the storms swirl around me. I will focus my eyes on you. You are my hope, my peace, my protection, my strength. In your presence is fullness of joy.*

For Further Reflection:

Joshua 23:14
Matthew 14:22–33
John 14:26–27

Day 78

"Repent, then, and turn to God, so that your sins may be wiped out, that times of refreshing may come from the Lord."

Acts 3:19 (NIV)

I am drawing my church back to myself. Many do not know me or call upon my name. Many know me, and yet it makes no difference in their lives. I remind my church to be holy, as I am holy. Know the difference between the sacred and the profane.

My people are not on earth to fit in but to mark the difference between light and darkness. It is time to call the church back to myself. My church has lost the ability to discern between good and evil. Many places are calling evil good and good evil, even in my church. My people are doing, saying, and watching things that are a shame to talk about. They take pleasure in them and no longer feel my Spirit grieving and telling them they are heading in the wrong direction.

I am issuing a trumpet call: "Come back to me, my people." Remember that my Word says, "Woe to those who call evil good, and good evil."[4] Evil is more than an activity. It is an attitude, a bent that is so deep that only my Holy Spirit can root it out. My people must learn once again to hate what I hate—to abhor it, not to take part or pleasure in it or flirt with it, but to abhor and depart from it.

I am calling all my intercessors to pray for my Spirit of conviction, a consciousness of sin, to fall over my church. If you want revival, this must come first. Just because evil prevails and grows stronger in the land, it does not mean my standards of good and evil have changed. My church must not compromise. My church must identify with my holiness.

Many hold back for fear of repercussions, but nevertheless, you must not compromise. If you do not discern a difference between the holy and the profane, you are not salt preserving the world. I have not yet given up on my church. I am calling them back to myself. Pray for a Spirit of conviction in yourself, your churches, and your country. Pray for the church to stand up for what they know is right, because the ones who do not stand for me will no longer walk with me.

---

4 Isaiah 5:20

Prayer: Lord, you are a holy God. Holy Spirit, I ask you to convict me of those things in my life that do not please you, the compromises I excuse. Thank you for already forgiving me. Through your Word, you show me how to align my thoughts with your nature. You guide me into your truth so we can discern good from evil. Show me how to pray for your church so we may be salt and light in this world.

For Further Reflection:

Isaiah 55:6–12
Matthew 5:13–16
2 Corinthians 6:16–7:1

Day 79

You, Lord, hear the desire of the afflicted; you encourage them, and you listen to their cry, defending the fatherless and the oppressed.

Psalm 10:17–18 (NIV)

Open your ears and listen. You will hear the cries of many little ones. Their cries come from pain, hurt, broken trust, and wounded hearts. Do you hear them cry? They are murdered, abandoned, used, and abused for convenience's sake—for money, power, and lust. No one realizes that they are becoming the instruments of the spirit of destruction in this land. You must listen. It is not enough to say, "Isn't that awful?" It is not enough.

As I allow each of you to hear their cries in your heart—the cries of the little ones throughout this land and the world—be faithful to pray. If I put them in your path, be instruments of healing. I have given you my spirit of wisdom and revelation. Their injury is so great that no one understands, and many do not live. Their blood cries out to me from your country and the world. I created them. I remember how carefully I planned each of their lives, and now they are not. Your land cries out to me for their blood because she has lost her children. You must reach out to stop this.

There is no child who is unwanted, who is not special, who is not planned, who is not loved, for I love them. They are mine. Pray. Let your heart break for these who are not yours because they are mine. They must know that their safety is in my name.

Prayer: *Lord, every child is precious to you—wanted, loved, created by you for your glory. Open the eyes of my heart to see their pain through your merciful and loving heart. Open my ears to hear their cries. Thank you for showing me how to love them and pray for them so they may receive healing and restoration for their wounded bodies and souls.*

For Further Reflection:

Psalm 34:18
Psalm 139:13–18
2 Corinthians 1:3–4

Day 80

"Teacher, which is the greatest commandment in the Law?" Jesus replied: "'Love the Lord your God with all your heart and with all your soul and with all your mind.' This is the first and greatest commandment."

Matthew 22:36–38 (NIV)

I call you to worship me and love me. I have already shown you I love you. I loved you by sending my Son to die on the cross for you. Love me by letting go of all that holds you. I am your treasure, your portion, and your all. You love me by allowing me to be your all, and by loving me with your whole heart, soul, and mind.

Every promise in my book that you thought was for others is for you. I care about the things you care about. If you draw close to me, you will find that the unimportant things in your life will fall away—some with minimal effort. The center of your life must be me.

I love all who bear my name. Without you, I ache. No one can take your place. I want you. Love me and want me too. I died for you so that my blood would give you access to me. Use that access. Do not despise the access I provided for you.

Prayer: Father, I am amazed that you love me and want me so much that you have given me access to you through the blood of your precious Son. I place in your loving care all those things that try to take hold of me. I exchange them for you—my treasure, my portion, my all. I love you, Lord.

For Further Reflection:

John 3:13–17
2 Corinthians 1:20–22
Ephesians 2:4–8

Day 81

He who did not spare his own Son, but gave him up for us all—how will he not also, along with him, graciously give us all things?

Romans 8:32 (NIV)

What have I done to you that you are afraid of me? What could I have done for you that I have not already done beyond sending my Son to die for you? I have blessed each of you with my presence, my care, and my bounty. I long for you to come and worship me in spirit and in truth. But instead, some of you draw away from me out of fear. You're afraid of what you will lose. You are afraid of what I may ask you to do, and so you will not approach me at all.

My heart longs and grieves for all of you. Can't you trust me? Haven't I proven over and over that I love you? I have not harmed you. I am not asking you to do anything except come to me. Let me hold you. Rest in me. Trust that my will for your life is filled with good things. If there is any hardship to endure, I will endure it with you. I will not leave or forsake you, for I long to be with you. I want you to return that longing for me.

I realize there are times we cannot draw apart alone, but you must realize that I am walking with you and you with me. I want the longing that fills my heart to fill yours. Even when you are busy, I want your longing to be with me, to rise strong. The time may not be right, but I want the longing to be there. I want to be close to you. If we are not close, it is not because I have drawn away from you. I love you, and I promise you that I will enable you to do all I ask of you.

Prayer: Lord, you long for us, your children, to draw near to you. May the longings of your heart fill my heart and draw me closer to you. As I come near, I experience your overwhelming love for me—a love that drives out all fear, a love that assures me I am your beloved child and you will never leave me or forsake me. May my trust in you grow, as I experience this love, until I know that I am your beloved child.

For Further Reflection:

Psalm 28:6–9
Isaiah 49:13–16
John 4:23–24

Day 82

Be shepherds of God's flock that is under your care, watching over them—not because you must, but because you are willing, as God wants you to be.

1 Peter 5:2 (NIV)

I ordained each person in my church to be fruitful and multiply. I ordained the places where each of you walks. In those places, there are people who know you, and whom I love and died for. I do not necessarily call you to talk to them about me, even though I may do so. But I call you to live your life with me in front of them and act on their behalf. If you do this, you will earn the right to speak. You may not need to speak to them, for their lives will change because of my presence in you and your care for them.

Remember that you are sheep, and sheep beget sheep. I remind you that those little lambs need shepherds. I am calling each one in my church to be an under-shepherd and take care of my little lambs. Some you will birth yourself, and some you will adopt. There are many orphans— bedraggled, sick, hungry, and hurt. Add them to your own flock if you come across them. Do not say, "This one is not mine. I am not responsible." Do what you can for the people around you, even little things that seem insignificant, and then you will see yet more you can do.

You must be willing to get dirty, bear the weight of another person's life, and spend yourself on behalf of others. Do not be like the hireling, who flees when he sees the wolf approaching. But be like David, who, when he saw the lion and the bear, stepped forth to defend the sheep. My power in him tore apart the lion and the bear that would take his father's sheep. Be willing to give your life for others, as I laid down my life for you.

The path David walked led to the fulfillment of his purpose: reigning as king. All of you have promises from me, and you are looking for a way to see those promises fulfilled. Follow David's example and do what is there for you to do. I will direct your steps. I will lead you into the promise I gave you just as I did for David. Remember, David's path led through many turns and twists before it led to the kingship that was his.

Do not be impatient or lose hope, for I direct your paths, your ways, and your steps. If you will be faithful in doing the things you know, take care of others, and show them who I am, then you will end up in the middle of that promise I gave you a long time ago. Be willing to take care of the things that are mine and the people who are mine, for I take care of you.

Prayer: *Lord, you call us to care for others with the heart of a shepherd—a shepherd who lays down their life for the sheep. Lead me to those you want me to defend, to care for, to aid. Teach me how to live my life before them in such a way that reveals who you are. Show me how to love and care for them with your shepherd's heart.*

For Further Reflection:

Matthew 9:35–38
John 10:11–16
Philippians 2:1–4

Day 83

I appeal to you, dear brothers and sisters, by the authority of our Lord Jesus Christ, to live in harmony with each other. Let there be no divisions in the church. Rather, be of one mind, united in thought and purpose.

1 Corinthians 1:10 (NLT)

Do not lean on your own understanding. Rely on me, and I will direct your paths. When the Enemy creates confusion around you, I will walk you straight through the confusion. He may throw up smokescreens so you can't see me, and you can't see what I am doing in and through you. But that does not mean I am not at work. You may lose a battle, but you will win the war. Do not despair. Mix your faith with patience, and trust me.

Do not carry the weight of your own lives or that of others. Lay it down. Give it to me. The darkness and weariness you may feel do not come from me. Remember who you fight against. Remember, you do not fight against each other. Learn to forgive as I have forgiven you. Let each other go so that I might bring you back together.

If my church is to be united, you must stop fighting each other and recognize that it is Satan who brings division. As he once divided my angels, so he tries to divide my church. Fight him by knowing I have given you strength and weapons mighty for the pulling down of strongholds. Fight him, knowing the gates of hell cannot prevail against you, my church, united and storming those gates. It is not hopeless. It is not beyond your strength, for you can do all things because I strengthen you.

Recognize your Enemy. Do not lay down the weapons I gave you. Do not give him an opportunity to hurt you. Stay under my blood and my righteousness. Outside of this, you are vulnerable. He is without mercy.

Prayer: Lord, you triumphed over the Enemy at the cross and granted me the privilege of walking in that victory with you. Teach me how to use the weapons you have given me—your Word, your Spirit, and the power of your blood. You have also given me forgiveness as a weapon. When I forgive others as you have forgiven me, the Enemy has no hold over me. Thank you for teaching me how to live from your new nature—a life rooted in your love, expressed through the fruit of your Spirit.

For Further Reflection:

2 Corinthians 10:3–5
Galatians 5:15–26
Ephesians 6:10–18

Day 84

But thanks be to God! He gives us the victory through our Lord Jesus Christ.

1 Corinthians 15:57 (NIV)

It is my grace in which you stand. It is my grace that will bring mountains down as you shout,

"Grace, grace," until the mountain becomes a plain. You are not alone. You do not have to defend in your own strength. You are not dealing with each other. Realize who your enemy is and realize there are more for you than against you.

I assure you victory and equip you with weapons that are mighty. I train your hands for war. I give you the tongue of the learned so you might speak words of wisdom and encouragement to the weak.

I fight for you as Captain of the hosts of heaven. You cannot lose. Lift your hands and praise me. Look beyond your circumstances and praise me. If I am for you, then who can be against you? I will cause you to stand in the day of adversity. When your strength is small and you are weak, I am strong.

Prayer: *I praise you, Lord! Thank you for fighting for me. You never abandon me or leave me to face trouble alone. You equip me and enable me to stand strong in the grace of your empowering presence. Victory is guaranteed.*

For Further Reflection:

2 Kings 6:15–17
Zechariah 4:6–7
Romans 8:31–39

Day 85

"When you pass through the waters, I will be with you; and when you pass through the rivers, they will not sweep over you. When you walk through the fire, you will not be burned; the flames will not set you ablaze."

Isaiah 43:2 (NIV)

My people, the storms will come. For some of you, the storm is here and has been here for some time. Do not be afraid. Remember, I am here with you in the middle of the storm. At no time during these storms have I said I was opposed to you. I am pleased with you, and I am for you. When I called Peter out of the boat to walk on the water, he believed he could do it.

Remember that the promises and the anointing I gave you long ago still stand. Keep your eyes on me. Remember, I am for you and not against you. If I have given my life for you, have I not also given grace for you to stand and be blameless in spirit, soul, and body? All I have promised and called you to do, you will do if you keep your eyes on me. Remember, I am your safety and protection in the midst of the storm. It is too strong for you to endure without my presence. My Word will hold you steady.

Prayer: *Lord, when waves of doubt, unbelief, or fear rise against me, I fix my eyes on you and not on the storm. You hold me steady by the truth of your Word. You are for me. Your presence never leaves me. With your unchanging love, you guide me safely through the storm. Thank you for your faithfulness.*

For Further Reflection:

Psalm 107:25–31
Romans 8:31–32
Hebrews 10:23

Day 86

Therefore, since we have been made right in God's sight by faith, we have peace with God because of what Jesus Christ our Lord has done for us.

Romans 5:1 (NLT)

Remember what I have done for you. Remember my death on the cross. My death canceled your attachment to sin and sin's attachment to you. My suffering and death bought freedom for you. Freedom from sin, sorrow, pain, grief, suffering, and the law. They took my body down from the cross and laid me in the tomb. What good could that be?

The body of sin, of your slavery, is laid in the grave, buried with me. You are no longer required to walk in that body. I went into hell and disarmed and defeated your enemies who kept you captive. I took the captives, my faithful, from them. I freed you from their influence and power. I rose again so you might rise and live in my life—in me. Then I ascended. My followers did not understand that I must leave so I could give you the Holy Spirit with his gifts. I did this so that as you live out my life, you will bear the fruit of the Spirit and display my power throughout the earth.

You are no longer in bondage to the old man, your old nature, sin, and the law. You are no longer in bondage, because of my blood shed on the cross. You are no longer at the mercy of emotion or sickness, because of the wounds on my back. You are no longer at the mercy of spiritual wickedness.

You are freed to live at peace in my Spirit, surrounded by my presence and the people I have sent to guide you, to tell you about me. Each of you has something that the others around you do not have. You must tell one another to come to unity of faith in the body. There is one Lord.

I have taken complete care of you in my death, burial, resurrection, and ascension. Think on these things and apply them to your life, and you will have peace and joy. Remember what I have done and meditate on these things.

Prayer: *Jesus, I am a new creation in you. By your blood shed on the cross, you defeated the Enemy who held me captive in sin. You freed me from the bondage of my old nature—sin, pain, and sorrow—and raised me up into a new life in you. Thank you for your Holy Spirit, who teaches me how to live in your love, joy, and peace, and walk with my brothers and sisters in unity.*

For Further Reflection:

Romans 6:3–11
2 Corinthians 5:17
Colossians 2:13–15

Day 87

You have been set apart as holy to the Lord your God, and he has chosen you from all the nations of the earth to be his own special treasure.

Deuteronomy 14:2 (NLT)

Are you ready to be holy? Are you ready to be set apart? Many of you have prayed, "Lord, make me holy, set me apart, consecrated unto you." But are you ready? Do you know that holiness and consecration mark you as different—targets of hatred and persecution? That is why I ask you if you are ready. Do you truly want to be holy? If you think that looking like me and acting like me will make you popular, look at my life, especially my crucifixion week. Being an object of my healings or being one of my disciples puts you in danger.

Are you sure you want me to heal you? When I came to the pool of Bethesda, I asked the man if he wanted to be healed because it would set him apart. He would not be the same. Many people thought I asked him because he was crippled, but I asked him because of the aftermath.

Many of you have asked me for things. Count the cost. The time is coming when those who are set apart for me will be different in many ways from those around them. Many will suffer tribulation and persecution. I have overcome the world, so do not be afraid of the tribulation.

I want you to know the cost of asking me to make you holy, set you apart, and make you mine. Without holiness, you cannot see me, and your eternity will be spent in darkness. To be holy is costly, and for some of you it will be more costly than others.

All who choose me follow the path of my cross at the risk of being different and hated. When the time comes, I will strengthen you. I want you to know the choice you must make. I chose you. Choose me. Lift me up on high so others may come to me.

Prayer: Lord, I am reminded of Peter's response when you gave him the choice to walk away. He declared that you are the Son of God and have the words of eternal life. Where would he go? Like Peter, I respond, "Where would I go?" You are the only way that leads to life—a life filled with joy in your presence that strengthens me, hope in adversity, and love that conquers all fear. I choose your way of holiness. I choose you.

For Further Reflection:

John 5:2–20
John 6:67–69
John 17:11–26

Day 88

"It is time to seek the LORD, until he comes and showers righteousness on you."

Hosea 10:12 (NIV)

All my people must seek me, my holiness, and my righteousness. Remember my words, "Blessed are they who hunger and thirst for righteousness, for they shall be filled."[5] I will place a hunger in each person, a hunger for my holiness and my presence. They will seek me and turn away from all that weighs them down and pulls them away from me. All who call on my name will feel drawn by the Holy Spirit to come close to me and be filled with my presence, my holiness, and my righteousness. They will be clean—without spot or wrinkle. All shall proclaim Jesus as Lord.

Focus on me. No longer focus on yourself or each other, and you will become all that you were created to be. Do not focus on yourself, but focus on the Father and his

5 Matthew 5:6, paraphrased

will. In this, we shall be one, for your focus will not be on the things of this world, on yourselves, or each other but on me. I live in all those who call themselves by my name. You will all be one. Barriers will come down. Wrinkles shall be erased, and spots disappear. My bride will exalt her God not because of what he has done for her but for who he is. She will have joy.

All my people will praise me from the rising of the sun to its setting. Throughout all the earth, my glory shall come down upon your land and your lives in a way you have never seen before. I love you, and you will let me love you. Resistance will dissolve, for nothing can stand before my glory.

Prayer: Lord, my heart seeks you—your holiness and righteousness. As I turn my eyes away from the things of the world, focus them on you and all that is holy. Thank you for your Holy Spirit's drawing me ever closer to you, deeper into your presence, where I am cleansed and made whole. I rejoice in the glory of your presence.

For Further Reflection:

Psalm 29:1–2
Ephesians 5:25–27
Colossians 3:1–4

Day 89

The Lord *is trustworthy in all he promises and faithful in all he does.*

Psalm 145:13 (NIV)

All my people throughout my church have received promises from me, written and personal. These promises are sometimes through my written Word that comes alive for you, a prophetic word, or from my Spirit deep within you. My church waits for my promises. The Enemy has come in and cast a veil of doubt, saying to you, just as he did to Eve in the garden, "Has God really said . . . ?"

Recall what I have done for you. Cast off doubt, despair, and the unbelief that the Enemy has spread over you. What I have said to you, I will do. Nothing is too hard for me. I am the God of all flesh. Nothing is too difficult for me.

Do not look at circumstances, but look to my Word. Praise me for my power. Pray for one another and for my church that your faith may rise, and the spirits of doubt, despair, and unbelief will be quenched and destroyed. Pray that you will trust me. I am a God who does not lie.

If I have given you my Son, should I not give you other things besides, especially what I promised you? Do not give in to doubt. Lift my Word high. Instead of questioning me, praise me. If you are honest, you will realize how many things I have done for you. Pray for your brothers and sisters that I may be lifted up.

Prayer: *Thank you, Lord, for your promises that you have made alive in my heart. Promises reminding me that nothing is impossible for you. Promises reminding me that you have not forgotten me. Promises I can stand on when circumstances would tempt me to give in to doubt or unbelief. Teach me how to stand on your Word in faith—for my own life and as I support my brothers and sisters.*

For Further Reflection:

Jeremiah 32:17
Mark 11:22–24
Hebrews 3:12–14

Day 90

"They will fight against you but will not overcome you, for I am with you and will rescue you," declares the LORD.

Jeremiah 1:19 (NIV)

Remember, my church, the Enemy knows his time is short, and he is angry. You may feel the effects of that anger, but only for a short time. He cannot destroy you. There is nothing you cannot stand against when I am in you. Stand up, resist, and he will flee, even in this time when his anger is rising and his time is short. There is nothing he can do that I cannot lift you out of.

There is no weapon formed against you that will prosper, no voice spoken against you that will succeed. Although the Enemy has power on earth for a time, he has no power over you. The Enemy brings illusion, not truth.

Stand firm, rooted in my grace. He cannot cause you to fall. You are my servant, and you will not fall. He will try to obscure what I am doing in my church. He is without hope and has laid his hopelessness upon my people. But my people will know the truth and know that I am God. When you feel his fury, you will not fall, for I will cause you to stand. You will feel it, but it will not overcome you.

Do not claim as your own the darkness, the blackness you may feel around you. The devil will flee, for he fears my presence in you just as he feared my presence in my Son when he was on earth in a human body. Just as the Enemy said he knew Paul and he knew Jesus, now he will say he knows you. I know each one of you. He knows he cannot stand before my presence in you, so do not fear him. Do not even give him notice. You may rejoice when you triumph over him. But rejoice that you take his place in heaven. Rejoice that you will live where he once lived and have the fellowship he once had. Rejoice in that. Rejoice in me.

Prayer: Lord, I rejoice because I am rooted and grounded in your love. I rejoice because you enable me to stand safe and secure in you. I rejoice because the Enemy has no power over me. I rejoice because I live in the joy of your presence. I rejoice that my name is written in heaven. I rejoice in you!

For Further Reflection:

Isaiah 54:17
Luke 10:17–20
Philippians 4:4

Afterword

Anna Joy seemed an unlikely candidate to be chosen by the Lord to be an intercessor, a hero of faith. Living with cerebral palsy, she carried both pain and joy. She faced hardship, loss, abuse, and betrayal. Yet her intimacy in Christ deepened, and her childlike faith opened the way to the presence of God, his provision, and miracles.

Later, as she experienced physical decline and her world grew smaller, the scope of her intercessory prayer widened. With wisdom and a surrendered heart, she believed God for the impossible.

She was a mentor, a spiritual mother, and a friend. Anna Joy was a gift from God to those who knew her. Her story is a legacy that continues to inspire—a contagious song of joy.

To learn more about Anna Joy, you can read her story: *Song of Joy: A Little Girl in the Hands of a Big God.*

*Anna Joy is a pseudonym to protect the privacy of those integral to her story.

Acknowledgments

My deep appreciation and gratitude to all those who have made this book possible.

Pastor Tess Brunmeier. Thank you for your wisdom and insight as you reviewed these devotions and for your heartfelt endorsement.

Mom (Luella Shawhan). You opened the door to the world of books for me. You began my journey of devotion to Jesus.

Intercessory Prayer Team. These devotions could not have been shared with the body of Christ without the power of intercessory prayer. I want to thank the faithful prayer warriors who continually lifted me up as I wrote. Your love, prayers, and unwavering support through the years mean more to me than words can express.

Friends of the Pen. I have learned so much from each of you as we've shared our writing journeys together. Anita Klumpers, Lori Lipsky, and Robin Steinweg—your guidance, encouragement, and friendship have shaped me into a better writer. I'm grateful for every word, every critique, and every moment we've spent growing together.

WordGirls. I am grateful for each of you in this amazing writing community mentored by Kathy Carlton Willis. Through our shared journey, we have not only developed our craft as writers but have also grown in faith—encouraging one another and lifting each other up in prayer.

Kathy Carlton Willis. I honestly can't thank you enough for all the mentoring, teaching, encouragement, brainstorming, networking, and wisdom you've poured into me. You've shown up with generosity and heart time and time again, and it's made such a difference in my life. I've grown so much because of your influence, and I'm incredibly grateful—not just for what you've taught me, but for who you are.

Michelle Rayburn. Thank you so much for your meticulous attention to detail in typesetting and editing my manuscript, as well as for the beautiful cover design. Your expertise and care have made a meaningful difference, and I'm truly grateful for your dedication in bringing my work to life.

To Our Lord Jesus Christ, I am deeply grateful for your divine hand in bringing forth these devotions. You knew exactly what I needed to grow in faith and understanding. I dedicate this work to your glory.

About the Author

Joanie Shawhan shares true-life stories, offering her readers an eyewitness view of the action. *Song of Joy: A Little Girl in the Hands of a Big God* and her Selah Awards finalist book, *In Her Shoes: Dancing in the Shadow of Cancer,* reflect the value of "your story plus my story become our stories." An ovarian cancer survivor and registered nurse, Joanie speaks to medical students in the Survivors Teaching Students program. Visit Joanie: www.joanieshawhan.com

"What a treasure this book is of God's love for us. Words of grace and truth. Words of comfort and conviction. Words pointing us to Jesus and bringing us closer to God. Each devotion is backed by Scripture. If you are seeking an authentic experience with the Holy Spirit, you will find him while reading and searching out the Scriptures. May God bless your time and draw you to the words you need to hear today."

—**Pastor Tess Gitter Brunmeier** (Vineyard Church USA) BS education, MA psychological counseling, MDiv, and PhD (ABD) church history

www.ingramcontent.com/pod-product-compliance
Lightning Source LLC
LaVergne TN
LVHW010655110826
845149LV00014B/3108

* 9 7 9 8 9 9 9 7 1 2 7 1 4 *